# Two Old Black Sticks

My Journey Into Irish Traditional Music

**John Kerr**

Copyright © 2013 John Kerr except as follows:

Lyrics from the song "When New York Was Irish" ©1987 Terence Winch, Green Linnet Music, BMI.

Essay material written by Mick Moloney from the 1997 Washington Irish Festival program book © 1997 National Council for the Traditional Arts, Silver Spring, MD.

Lyrics from the songs "Andrew Rose" and "Slievenamon" are Traditional, Public Domain.

Previously unpublished article by Bob Hickey © 1993 Greater Washington Ceili Club, Washington, DC.

Washington Irish Folk Festival program book covers and material from 1986 through 1996 © 1986-1996 by Greater Washington Ceili Club, Washington DC.

Washington Irish Folk Festival program book covers and material from 1997 through 2000 © 1997-2000 by National Council for the Traditional Arts, Silver Spring, MD.

Inside front cover photograph © 2011 by P. Brennan's Irish Pub, Arlington, VA.

All other photographs are from the personal collection of the author.

Dancing in O'Shea's Merchant Pub, Dublin, July 1987.
Partner and photographer unknown.

Session at P. Brennan's Pub, Arlington, Virginia,
March 2011. Lee Marsh on bodhran. P. Brennan's photo.

# An Audience with the Pope

It showed up in my Facebook inbox late on the last Sunday night of the year, a seemingly innocuous invitation. A mere seventeen words, yet with layers of meaning conveyed within it. I felt a bit like some obscure campaign worker who'd just received an invitation to a White House State Dinner, or a lowly cleric summoned to a private audience with the Pope himself.

**Brendan Mulvihill** December 26, 2010 at 8:52pm
Subject: New Year's Eve Session
Hello Friends,
Would anyone like to have a tune at my house on New Year's Eve?
Brendan

Being invited to socialize with Brendan Mulvihill – although certainly no everyday occurrence for me – was not really a surprise. I had known Brendan for a good quarter century. I first met him when he was the brilliant fiddler playing alone on stage in the decaying Spanish Ballroom in the even more decrepit Glen Echo Park where I was taking my first introductory classes in Irish set dancing. I was trying to learn the strange up-on-the-down-beat Clare dance step and the figures of the Caledonian Set. *House. House at home. In your own place.* I can still hear Mike Denney's voice telling us over and over again what to do as we stumbled around the floor. I thought I was taking those classes to learn to dance, and eventually that's what I did. But what I didn't realize then was that I was also taking my first steps into a new world, a new culture, indeed a new community. I was beginning a journey into the world of Irish traditional music, one that continues to this day.

That journey has led me to many places, some that are real and others that are – as is said of the music-rich Sliabh Luachra region between Cork and Kerry – states of mind. (The ones that are states of mind tend to make me want to linger longer than the real ones do, I've found.) First I was learning to dance, just hoping that whenever I approached a potential partner at the ceili she'd recognize me from the class and remember that I sort of knew the step and wouldn't be tromping all over her toes. Eventually I got pretty good at it. (The dancing, not the toe tromping.) Then I found myself volunteering at the Irish Folk Festival at Glen Echo Park, the same place I was going to dance. I ended up more and more involved with the festival as years passed, helping to shape the program and plan it out during the months of preparation each year. I was booking bands, writing program notes and ferrying performers around from place to place. I joined the Greater Washington Ceili Club, ending up on the board of directors, booking and running the monthly ceili, helping to find new venues and organizing and attending events at far-flung places all over the east coast of America and in Ireland.

As I journeyed and evolved in my newfound community, I met, got to know and even became friends with both the alpha citizens and the ordinary foot soldiers of the world of Irish traditional music and dance, from both sides of the pond. It is indeed a large and far-flung family, as I discovered early on, and I was happy to have found myself in it and happy with my place in it. But almost from the beginning I realized I was harboring a deep secret. I loved listening to the music, I loved dancing to it, but what I *really* wanted to do was play it myself. So I got a flute and I started learning. I sought teaching wherever I could find it, even though there was no one I knew of teaching Irish flute around home. Eventually I started going to sessions, where I learned a lot and had tons of fun – but not without some pain as well. (I also came to learn that's part of the process.) I got over the hurdles of playing in tune, learning the tunes by ear, having a tune I could play all the way through without collapsing when someone said *John, give us a tune,* and finally being able to start a tune set on my own at a session and drive it all the way through to the end. I spent a lot of time playing music, by myself and with others, even getting paid for it on the extremely rare occasion. (And I'm not just saying that to throw the IRS off my scent.) Perhaps others in the vast Irish music family were even starting to think of me as a musician, not all those other labels I'd had over the years. But, as is often said, we're always hardest on ourselves. And so it was that after 20 years of playing the flute I still wasn't sure that *I* thought of myself as a musician.

Which is why that little New Year's invitation from Brendan Mulvihill hit me the way it did. Here was one of the great musicians in all of Irish music, someone who had known me even before I had a flute, inviting me over to have a tune. Perhaps I *am* a musician after all. And if that's true, it means that even though my journey into the world of Irish traditional music has not yet reached its destination (and hopefully won't for a good long while) for sure it has hit a significant milestone. Actually that had probably been true for a while, but if not for being jarred by that little Facebook invitation I wouldn't have known it – or admitted it, anyway.

As it happened, there was actually more talking, drinking, eating and general conviviality than there was music that night at Brendan's house. Such is often the way when Irish musicians gather for a tune. Terry Winch was one of the other musicians who was there that night.

I have known Terry as long as I've known Brendan. He and his band Celtic Thunder were the house band at the very first ceilis I ever went to, back when I was first learning to dance the sets in the Spanish Ballroom. One of the first things I came to know about Terry was that both he and his brother and band-mate Jesse Winch had migrated to Washington from New York City in the 1970s, bringing the seed of what would become Washington's Irish traditional music scene with them. (They were joined in that by Brendan Mulvihill and Billy McComiskey who I have had the privilege of knowing ever since the days I first discovered the music, and by others like Lou Thompson and Peggy Riordan who I unfortunately never had the chance to meet.) In addition to playing the D/C# box in Celtic Thunder, Terry Winch is a gifted poet and songwriter who often focuses his written work on recollections of his life as an Irish American and an Irish musician. It was around the time I first met Terry that his best-known work emerged, a song called *When New York Was Irish* that was sung by Laura Murphy on Celtic Thunder's album *The Light of Other Days*. (The royalty checks he's been cheated out of on pirated versions of this song alone would have surely been enough for him to live out every musician's dream and quit the day job.)

*I'll sing you a song, of days long ago,*
*When people from Galway and the County Mayo.*
*From all over Ireland came over to stay,*
*And take up a new life in Amerikay.*

*They were ever so happy, they were ever so sad,*
*To grow old in a new world, through good times and bad.*
*All the parties and weddings, the ceilis and wakes,*
*When New York was Irish, full of joy and heartbreaks.*

In this song, and in much of his less-pilfered work, Terry is recounting his journey from within a world filled with Irishness, and all that Irishness brings with it – music, dance, joy, pain, love, heartbreak, and a wealth of character and characters – out to the world at large. He's telling us how he became a traditional musician in the traditional way. Which happens to be the direct opposite of the journey I've been taking, from a life of no Irishness (despite the somewhat diluted Irish blood that courses within my veins) to an immersion in things Irish, particularly the music. I too have known parties, weddings, ceilis and wakes, but for me they have been the means of inclusion in a world that I didn't even know existed until I was already an adult and stepping into it. If I'm now a traditional musician –and I sometimes like to think that I am – then I've become one in a most untraditional way. And while they are by no means profound, I have my own stories that I've gathered along the way. Stories that might be of some interest to someone, even if it's only me when I look back on them in my dotage. So here they are in print, for what it's worth. At the end of his book *That Special Place: New World Irish Stories,* Terry Winch has a word with all those who may not have liked *When New York Was Irish* for whatever reason. He says: *Write your own version.* Well, I like his song. But I'm writing my own version anyway.

# The Session

*Approximations
Of Irish tunes. Some are close,
But too many aren't.*

Some seven or eight years after I started going there, conditions at the Nanny O'Brien's session had gotten so bad that the regulars started writing haiku about it – and in particular the depths to which it had sunk – as a way of blowing off steam. Why did we resort to an ancient Japanese poetic art form to vent our frustration about the state of Irish traditional music in the capital of the United States? Because we were trying to promote cross-culturalism in an era of political correctness? Nope. Because Irish traditional music is, in fact, big in Japan? Nah. Because our favorite before- or after-session place to chow down, conveniently located just a few doors down Connecticut Avenue from Nanny's, was a sushi restaurant called Spices? Not really. It actually started after Tes Slominski, a great fiddler from down in central Virginia who hovered around the DC session scene off and on for years before going off to grad school in Limerick to seek fame and fortune as an ethnomusicologist, sent around one of those joke-filled chain e-mails that was called "Gig Haiku." Things like *An oxymoron: / "He played the accordion / With delicacy"*. Or *I once had a dream / Big house, new car, big money / Now I play the bass*. Or my personal favorite, *My drummer helped me / Count the syllables*. Someone (it was probably me) got that e-mail from Tes, went to town on it and sent out another e-mail called "Session Haiku" – of which the one reproduced above was one of the few that didn't explicitly call out the guilty parties by name in the most vicious of fashion. (If you want to know about *A three Bob night* you'll have to ask me in person. I'm not writing it here.) A spate of round-robin e-mail hilarity ensued that generated several dozen haiku from various folks and lasted for about a week, until we all started crying in our beer again.

But I'm getting way ahead of myself here. What has always been known as "the session" in DC – almost like it's a living, breathing, tangible thing, which actually it pretty much is – had been going on for well over a decade before I ever stumbled into it. Started sometime in the 1970s, I think, around or shortly after Billy McComiskey, Brendan Mulvihill and Andy O'Brien began their epic and legendary run as The Irish Tradition in the Dubliner pub on Capitol Hill. Dennis Botzer, who everyone calls Doc for reasons I've never known, was around even then, and when pressed he can put together a biblical list of who begat whom to describe the session's progression from pub to pub around town. Indeed he did that once, to Mick Moloney for an essay Mick wrote in the program book for the Wolf Trap Irish Festival in 1997.

*It started in 1978 in the Dubliner with Brendan Mulvihill and Billy McComiskey leading the way. Then musicians started up another session at Ellen's Irish Pub. After Ellen's closed the session moved to The Tavern, which was known as the "Zoo Bar" because it was located on Connecticut Avenue just beside the Zoo. That lasted about a year. Then it moved to Kelly's Irish Times on "F" St beside the Dubliner, again for about a year. Then Brendan Mulvihill and another local fiddler Terry O'Neill started a session at the Brown Derby, located across the street from the Four Provinces pub on Connecticut Avenue. Again that lasted about a year. Then it moved back once more to Kelly's Irish Times and then back again to the Zoo Bar. It then moved to Brentwood for a few weeks to a pub called Kerry's Dairy and from there to Caffney's Pub in a "dicey neighborhood in the Northwest." From there it moved to Bosco's in Silver Spring and musicians gathered there for over two years on Wednesday nights. That ended when the pub burned down! After that there were what Dennis described as "rotating house sessions" for a while before a regular pub session started again at Hagan's Four Courts in Rockville. That lasted for a couple of years before the current major session in the area started at Nanny O'Brien's at 3319 Connecticut Avenue in April 1993.*

At Nanny O'Brien's the nomadic session finally settled in for a good long run, a run that is still going on today, more or less (but mostly less.) Nanny O'Brien's is just up the street from the Zoo (and the Zoo Bar, where the session had hovered for a while during its exile), and just like the Brown Derby pub mentioned in the session genealogy it sits across the street from Ireland's Four Provinces (a pub that has always been called the Four P's by anyone who's ever set foot in it – even after they changed the name to Ireland's Four Fields or some such nonsense a few years ago.) Indeed, since the strip of storefronts across the street from the Four P's currently houses no pub called the Brown Derby, it's entirely possible that the Brown Derby sat in the same space then that houses Nanny O'Brien's now. At the very least, it was nearby – and with the Zoo Bar also nearby, it means that this couple of blocks on Connecticut Avenue is an important spot in the history of Irish sessions in Washington. If nothing else, it's where I entered the scene when I first walked into Nanny O'Brien's carrying a flute in my hand. As near as I can remember, it was a Wednesday night in early November 1995.

If you walked into Nanny O'Brien's now it would look much the same as it did that night I walked in almost twenty years ago. The giant flat screen TV that's replaced the old tube box at the end of the bar would catch your eye right away, of course, but aside from that it's still a long narrow room with the bar taking up most of the right side and the tiny stage and tables on the left, with about a six foot wide walkway right down the middle. The walls are stained wood that would be described as "distressed" by a store like Pottery Barn so as to jack up the price, and they're covered by the same sort and same massive quantity of kitschy objects d'art as you find in fine establishments like TGI Friday's. Except that the kitsch on Nanny's walls isn't factory-made by slaves in China like the stuff on those chain restaurants' walls. It's the real thing. Irish road signs stolen from all over the publican Brian Gaffney's native Kerry and smuggled to America in checked bags on an Aer Lingus flight. Posters from some event that took place years ago that have been framed, but not to museum-quality standard, so they're faded and yellow now behind the dirty and often cracked glass of the frame. And hanging on the wall behind the tiny stage are a ragged fiddle, banjo and guitar. In the heyday of Nanny's, while Brian was still there, you'd think the banjo and guitar were unplayable until Brian would pluck one of them off the wall to play along with whoever was getting paid to provide the music that night. The floor is a hard tile, so hard that no pint glass ever dropped on it could possibly escape breaking, and the lights even at mid-day are kept low – mainly to keep patrons from seeing what dangers may lurk on those floors, be they stray shards of glass that escaped the cursory sweep-up after the last breakage, or all manner of roaches or even worse forms of vermin that lurk in the crevices. Indeed the only time of day when the lights are cranked up to full strength is closing time, the time when publicans on the other side of the pond would yell *Time, gentlemen, time!* or

*Have you no homes to go to?* Such relatively tame means of emptying a bar clearly don't work in America, but flooding the place with enough light to illuminate a crime scene is apparently enough to sober the drunks up sufficiently for the ride home. And if that doesn't do it, the frightening *whoosh!* as the various vermin scurry back to their hiding places to escape the bright light surely will.

Passing between the not one, but two ladies rooms at the far end of the front room (Nanny O'Brien's, an early adapter of "potty parity"?), you enter the back room that has always been the home of the session. Not quite as deep as the front room, the back room's hard floor and relative openness make it a great space for music, as long as the only people in there are musicians. Once more than a handful of chattering drinkers come in, though, it's terrible. But such is true of pretty much every session venue I've ever seen, except that there are some that always sound terrible, no matter what. And a crowd of appreciative punters is something that always makes a session better than it would be otherwise, even if the music is drowned out.

The layout of the back room has changed just a bit over the years. The piano that was in the left front corner got moved to the right on the other side of the entrance and replaced by a built-in corner bench. Then the piano got moved out entirely to be replaced by a booth in the right front corner. The stack of kegs in a niche on the right side wall got covered over by a door. And once the District of Columbia passed the ban on smoking in bars, the cigarette machine on the back wall disappeared. But the one constant in that room from then 'til now is the two dartboards on the left side wall toward the back, always accompanied by persons chucking darts at them, with one exception. A sign on the wall by the boards absolutely forbids the throwing of darts after 8:00 pm on Monday nights, on account of the session – a rule for which every single one of the many session offenders who have come into Nanny's over the years is no doubt profoundly grateful.

The men's room at Nanny's deserves a special mention. I wouldn't exactly call it dirty, in the way a gas station restroom invariably is, but I wouldn't exactly call it clean either. Actually, except on the most rowdy of nights the floors, walls and fixtures are at least passable, albeit far from pristine. But I have never, ever, not even once seen the urinals flush. Oh, you can push down the handle when you're done, but the pool of yellow liquid never stirs. Yet somehow even with hard drinkers making a steady stream of deposits over the course of an evening, the bowls never overflow. I could never figure out how the staff got them to do that, nor did I ever learn how much the payoff to the health inspectors needed to be to keep the place open. After all, the men's room is the closest physical space in the whole building to the tiny kitchen in back. (And despite this, if you do ever eat at Nanny's I can recommend the turkey sandwich – giant slabs of freshly carved meat – or the Nanny Burger.)

Shortly after the attacks of September 11th, the urinals at Nanny's were each augmented with those rubber sieve-like things that prevent cigarette butts and chewing gum from being flushed down. Two things were notable about this. First, the urinals at Nanny's *didn't flush*. Second, the rubber thingies featured the likeness of Osama bin Laden, which allowed all of us true American men to fulfill our patriotic duty while relieving ourselves. (Also, I guess if someone ever spent an evening drinking at Nanny's but refused to use the jacks you could nab him as a terrorist.) But then after a few months I went in and noticed that the urinal screens were gone. I secretly pitied the poor Nanny's employee who had drawn the terrible assignment of reaching down into the yellow pools to pull them out. Walking out, I happened to run into Brian Gaffney and so I said *I see you took Osama out of the urinals*. To which he replied *We did?*

But all of the physical charms of Nanny O'Brien's wouldn't have made the place worth a second visit, if not for the people I encountered there that first night and on many nights to follow. Again, Mick Moloney's essay tells the tale.

*The proprietor of Nanny's is Brian Gaffney. Brian hails from Tralee, County Kerry and has been a resident of the DC area since 1993. He is a singer and also a tenor banjo and guitar player. He moved from Ireland to Boston in 1985 and finally got into the business of bar ownership, establishing Nanny's in 1993 after years of performing in pubs. He is one of only two traditional musicians in the United States who owns an Irish bar (the other is fiddler Tommy McCarthy who owns the Burren pub in the Boston area).*

*Brian loves having traditional music in Nanny's. On weekends he has stage acts but a traditional music session takes place in the bar every Monday and a music and set dancing session every Wednesday. The Monday night session takes place 52 weeks a year without fail. The session usually begins around nine and might finish around midnight. If the music is really flying the session might go on until one – maybe later. Some of the regulars who show up include Matt Shortridge and Kathy O'Rourke, Dennis and Angela Botzer, Mark Hillmann, David Abe, Danny Noveck, Charlie MacVickar, Sue Richards, Karen Ashbrook, Tom Donohue, Jim Curtin, Jennifer and Joshua Culley,*

*Orion Weiss, Betsy O'Malley, Rick Ryder, Tina Eck, Bill Buick, Nick Smiley, Brook Portner, Paul Norton, John Kerr and Drew Riggs. And musicians like Brendan Mulvihill, Myron Bretholz, Billy McComiskey, Philippe Varlet, Drew Hillmann, Mary Duke Smith, Kieran O'Hare, Zan McLeod and Linda Hickman might show up too as well as groups and musicians touring from Ireland - the likes of Seamus Begley, Steve Cooney and Altan. As Brian says "you never know who's going to walk in."*

Fifteen years on from when Mick wrote those words, it's amazing how many of those names are still part of the music here, and therefore part of my life. Brian is still here, and so is Nanny's, although Brian's family sold the pub to a new group of owners a few years back. In theory there is still a Monday night session there, but from what I hear the approximation of Irish music in it is miniscule at best. Several of the folks mentioned by Mick have left the area, although ironically in this new world of Facebook I often see more of them now than I did when they were living nearby. (Although the "have a tune" app isn't available in the App Store yet, so the virtual meetings aren't nearly as much fun as the real-life ones were.) Jim and Jennifer Curtin moved to Vermont, Josh Culley married Misa Acox and they moved to Tennessee. Drew Hillmann has been living in Ireland for years. Bill Buick moved to Philly, and Paul Norton moved out west somewhere, I think. Danny Noveck moved away and then came back and now has moved away again. Matt Shortridge and Kathy O'Rourke moved to a small town in Wisconsin, where from all indications they are living the dream life. But losing Matt was perhaps the worst blow the session scene here ever took. Others have just disappeared from the scene, like Tom Donohue, Nick Smiley, Brook Portner and Drew Riggs. Charlie

MacVickar and Myron Bretholz are pretty much up in Baltimore these days, although we see them every now and then. Others that Mick mentioned, like Kieran O'Hare, Linda Hickman and Billy McComiskey, lived in DC long ago but even when Mick wrote that were already out-of-towners who we were (and are) always glad to see. But everyone else on the list is still around, although due to kids, marital split-ups, gigs and day jobs (amazingly, it *is* possible to play music and have one of those) we may not see them out often enough.

So we have a solid core of players here still, that's been augmented by several stalwarts who have arrived since Mick wrote his piece. Rob Greenway came to town (and for a while was joined by his Roaring Mary band-mates Tes, Sara and Paddy) and now he runs a session at a dive bar in Rockville that I never go to because it's at the godawful hour of ten o'clock Saturday *morning*. Patrick Cavanagh showed up and travels the gig and session circuit with Doc. A couple of years ago he was joined by the lovely Crystal Bailey, and together they manage to prove that if you put enough banjos together it is indeed possible to make music. Those young bucks Josh Dukes and Brendan Bell are ubiquitous, and often joined by Sean McComiskey and Matt Mulqueen who are around so much you'd think they lived here too, even though they don't. Peter Brice, Spencer Nitchie and Jim Mahshie come all the way in from Annapolis. Diana Havlin is here, as is Lori Brent (and I think Lori was here back then, too, but somehow got left off Mick's list). We have new players who were in elementary school when I first came to Nanny's, like Kelly Criscuolo-DeButts whose list of talents, musical and otherwise, is longer than her name. And a couple of old guys like me who have been in town for a long time but only came to the music recently are doing a lot to make up for lost time. Keith Carr has joined with Tina Eck to form a band called Lilt that has already released two CDs and opened for Altan at the Birchmere, and Mitch Fanning is shepherding a whole new generation of fiddlers into Irish music and running a highly successful summer school every July. I'm sure there are some others who have slipped my mind at the moment, and when they read this they'll resent me for life. It's really a much more healthy session scene now than it was when I walked into it, and the standard of play around here has never been higher. Still, though, there was a lot already going on when I came into the music. More than I could ever have guessed....

*Tina starts to play*
*Seven flutes take up the tune*
*Damn, Mark's pipes are loud!*

When I started coming to Nanny's, I had been playing the flute for five or six years, although the first couple of those years would more accurately be described as "playing at" the flute rather than making music with it. The learning curve for the flute is steep, although not as steep as the "seven years practicing, seven years futzing with your reed, seven years playing" (or whatever it is) that it takes to call yourself a piper. (Although you could make up a saying for flutes that includes "seven years on Patrick Olwell's waiting list" and you wouldn't be far from the mark.) At any rate, I thought I could play well enough and knew enough tunes that it was time I started trying to play with others. I eased into it by going not to the Monday night session at Nanny's but instead to the Wednesday night "dance session" which was held in the front room. There I at least knew some of the players (and more importantly they knew me) from my years dancing the sets. And if ever the tunes got too obscure for me to play along, I could always grab a partner and dance. This strategy worked well for me and I became a regular on Wednesday nights for about a year and a half. But then Brian pulled the plug on the dance session, and I had no other choice but to join the crowd on Monday nights. This was truly going from the frying pan into the fire.

On a Monday night you could walk in the front door of Nanny O'Brien's at around nine o'clock, spy the few people sitting at the bar watching Monday Night Football, and swear the place was empty. But if you walked to the end of the bar and peered into the back room, you'd see that it was packed. The relatively small walkway between front and back not only hid the view of what was going on back there until you were right on top of it, it also contained the sound. Once you wormed your way in, you'd see a mob of musicians seated in roughly concentric arcs around the piano in the corner to the left, with every square inch not taken up by a musician occupied by someone there to drink and listen to the music – usually but not always in that order. Except on really crowded nights, there would be a narrow pathway kept open down the middle to allow access to the jacks and for waitresses to bring food orders up front, but there were also many times when a guy from the bar up front would need to do a Moses-parting-the-Red-Sea just to take a leak. This was quite a change for me from the quiet Wednesday nights that attracted only three or four players and a full set of eight dancers, if they were lucky. (Hmmm. Maybe that had something to do with why Wednesdays got cancelled.) At the Monday night session musicians got two free pints, and you qualified for that if all you could do was hold an instrument in your lap. But there was a definite pecking order to where you got to sit. Spots in the inner circle were reserved for the best players, those that had been coming the longest, or for their friends. Otherwise, seats were first come, first served, and that's where I fit in. Many was the night that I'd find myself sitting in the back row in front of the stack of kegs, and there were times I'd be sitting *on* a keg.

The inner circle was not just where the cool kids got to sit, it was where the music happened. There it was decided what the next tune would be, when the change would come, and even whether it was time yet for a new tune at all. As Matt Shortridge would often say, when a set of tunes is over you've got to let it breathe. You don't just jump right in with a new tune. But how long do you wait? That was a mystery only the folks in the inner circle understood. For the rest of us sitting in the back on a keg, playing at the session was like playing along with a CD – except that thanks to the crowded back room we were playing in, it was a CD being played on a really crappy CD player with a ton of fuzz in the speakers. So the first hurdle was figuring out what tune was being played. Did I know it? More importantly, did I know it well enough to join in, and at the speed they were playing it? I quickly realized that the hurdle of learning to play at a session was a hell of a lot higher than the hurdle of playing in my living room. If nothing else, there were a lot more people around me to be annoyed by my playing than just my neighbors who had to put up with what was leaking nightly through the thin walls between my condo and theirs.

This was not my first exposure to playing music in a sizeable ensemble. I spent my high school years as a band geek, playing the clarinet. I was pretty good at it, too, ending up as the first chair clarinet in the band my senior year and making all-regional. In fact, the main reason I chose the flute as my instrument when I decided to try playing Irish music was that the wooden flutes played in Ireland looked a lot like clarinets. How hard could that be? After all, the fingering part should come back pretty quickly and all I'd need to learn is how to make the sound by blowing into a hole instead of across a reed. After having at it for several years, that was proving to be the case – at least as long as I was in the privacy of my own home. At the session, I ran into two huge obstacles that had never been musical challenges for me before: sheet music and tuning.

There are some people that will tell you it's okay to use sheet music in Irish music. Those people are right, but only partially. Of course you should never, ever, under any circumstances show up at session with sheet music. That was patently obvious to me from the very first time I ever saw a group of Irish traditional musicians play. (But then again, what do I know? When I first started set dancing, I never saw anyone at a ceili checking the written instructions before dancing a set, either here or in Ireland. And I most certainly never saw a ceili with someone calling the dances, like they do at American square dances. Now both those things are commonplace, but if you ask me they're still abominations.) However, I did think it was okay to use sheet music as a learning aid. Otherwise, what was the deal with all those tunebooks, like O'Neill's? And being an old band guy, I was good with the notes and good with sight reading, so I thought that would be my quickest shot at getting a repertoire of tunes under my belt. If only there had been a flute teacher in town to set me straight, but despite the popularity of the flute in the DC area (that haiku above commemorates a session that was not at all atypical) the closest teachers I knew of were Frank Claudy and Chris Norman in Baltimore, and that was just too far from my suburban Virginia home. How was I to know that whatever dots I came across for that tune they played last night at the session, which I would find after an exhaustive search through the tune books on my shelves and the still primitive Internet, would be at best not quite the same setting played at Nanny's, or at worst flat out wrong? I always felt that I was one step behind everyone else on learning the tunes. But every once in a while, a tune would come along that I actually had under my fingers, so I'd pick up the flute and start to play. Only to hit brick wall number two, the big one. Tuning.

Some people would tell you that Irish trad music is folk music, and folk music not only doesn't need to be played in tune, it's actually better and more authentic if it's not. Those people would be wrong. (And more often than not, they'd be people who can't play in tune themselves.) Oh, it's true that Irish music isn't bound to the even-tempered twelve tone scale that pervades Western classical music, and that there are a few notes like C natural and F natural that are only rarely played true to the standard A440 tuning. And it's perfectly okay if your man the old fiddler can't hit the notes quite right any more, because there's still massive soul (or what the Irish would call *gra* or *nyah*) in his playing. The horrible clueless piano accompaniment on the old Michael Coleman 78 recordings can even be forgiven, to a point. He couldn't have known any better. But beyond that, whenever two or more are gathered together to play Irish music, good tuning must be in their midst. And that's the truth. Thing is, though, that's much easier said than done.

I never had any problem playing the clarinet in tune in my high school band days. Almost every day before rehearsal, and definitely before we went on stage for a concert, the band director would turn on this giant strobe tuner and go around the room having everyone play a concert Bb. (Why bands tune to Bb and orchestras tune to A I never did learn.) *Flat, push in. Sharp, pull out.* With over 50 kids in the band, that process took a while, but it did end up with us all at least in the same ballpark. From there, all that was required was that you continued to play in tune with everyone else as you wandered your way through the notes on the printed score, which for me wasn't ever an issue. So I thought I had the tuning thing licked, that is until I walked into the Monday night session at Nanny O'Brien's.

Although strobe tuners had, over the 25 years since I was in the high school band, shrunk in size from being bigger than a breadbox to being smaller than a pack of cigarettes, and even though I had one, I quickly discovered that it was useless at the session. I could blow into the flute either before I left home or when I got to the pub, pull the slide out to a perfect A440, and it did no good. I'd still be out of tune. It took a while to figure out why. Part of it was just the vagaries of the flute, which goes sharp or flat depending on how hard you blow it or how warm or cold it is, but the biggest reason was that I didn't know that playing in tune at an Irish session doesn't mean playing at A440. I came to learn that there are instruments like accordions and pipes that can't adjust their tuning on the fly. It is what it is, and everyone else in the session just has to live with it and adjust accordingly. (Oh why couldn't I have picked one of *those* instruments to play?) Tuning to the instrument that couldn't change replaced tuning to the strobe tuner, but unfortunately there was no dial or digital readout for that. It had to be done by ear. It helped that the fixed-pitch instrument at Nanny's was usually Mark's pipes, which besides being one of the best-played instruments in the session were also the loudest. By far. If you happened to be sitting next to Mark, you could be in tune or out of tune with him, but you'd never know it because you couldn't hear a note you were playing – until he decided to step away for a smoke, a chat or a drink. Then, as soon as the next tune started, you were exposed. Out of tune. Such was my lot and indeed, I fear, my reputation at the session. Things would get testy over tuning at times, although never to the point of blows, but usually it was just the constant cloud of insecurity hanging over my head. Maybe I felt that way because of something I heard Mick Moloney say once, when he was giving a lecture somewhere, about the whole notion of "Ireland of the Welcomes" in general, and sessions in particular. The visitor can come, commit all manner of sins and transgressions against the common good, and never know it. *They won't say anything,* Mick had said, *but they'll talk about you after you leave.* Well, maybe just so they wouldn't have the chance to talk about me, despite it often being a source of frustration or sometimes even pain, I kept going back to Nanny's on Monday night. And after I had been doing that for a while – not a short while, mind you, I'm talking years here – I found out something that Mick hadn't said. If you keep coming back long enough, eventually they will come to accept you as one of their own.

*Harmonica dude*
*Breakfast Band tambourine man*
*Brian threw them out*

*We played on in back*
*Chelsea Clinton sat up front*
*Brian scared her out*

There's a concept that you hear batted around a lot if you hang around with Irish musicians, although you're never really going to get a good definition of it unless you happen upon a little book by Barry Foy called *Field Guide to the Irish Music Session*. Session etiquette. It's a subtle and arcane thing, complex and yet simple. It's part of the answer to the question *Who's in charge here?* In most regular sessions, there's typically a person or two designated as the session host, and usually they get paid some small pittance by the pub to show up every week and run the session. Enforcing session etiquette thus falls upon the host, and oft times the session takes on the personality of its host in matters of choice of tunes, standard of play and the like. But Nanny O'Brien's was always, for better or worse, a session that had no host. Whoever showed up for the session could play in the session, no questions asked.

The closest thing that Nanny O'Brien's ever had to an arbiter of session etiquette was its proprietor, Brian Gaffney, who on occasion would take down the banjo that hung behind the stage in the front room and come into the back room to sit in, always having a prime seat opened up for him the moment he stepped foot in the room. But he was never there more than every few weeks at best. I do remember one night he was in residence, though, sitting next to me with his banjo and guitar. This would have been around Christmas 1998, I suppose. Early on, before too many musicians had arrived, Brian's first-grade daughter Kelly was about, with a set of exceedingly loud jingle bells in honor of the season. That brought to mind the time that someone had crossed the line by bringing a tambourine to the session and playing it, obnoxiously. Brian walked up to him and said *Get out. Now.* No questions asked, the guy was gone.

Later in the evening, Brian left the session to go up to the front room of the pub. He came back after a bit, and told us that while he was up front, he had noticed some young ladies sitting near the door, with cups of coffee they'd brought in from Starbucks across the street. As Brian said *They looked awful young*. He went up to them and to gently suss them out he said *Ladies, we* do *serve coffee here*. They were apparently very apologetic and immediately left the pub. Only then did Brian notice that one of the young ladies was Chelsea Clinton. We in the back room played merrily on through all this, totally oblivious to our "brush with greatness."

Other than Mr. Tambourine Man, I can only recall two other musicians (and I use that term very, very loosely; indeed I disrespect it in the worst possible way, now that I think of it) who were asked, or rather forced, by Brian to leave the session. One was the guy who showed up with an electric bass complete with amp. That conveniently thwarted our subtle attempts to deny him a seat, since he used the amp to park his butt. Rather than playing accompaniment like you'd expect a bass player to do, the guy started to thump out tunes. He left without a whimper when Brian asked him to – about halfway through his first attempted tune. The other guy who got tossed, an unfortunate fellow with a harmonica, actually got a bit of a raw deal, although none of us stood up in his defense. When he first took the harmonica out and started to play it, Brian was in the back room and told him in no uncertain terms that he was welcome at the session, but not if he played the harmonica. Then Brian left for the front room, and with the guy sitting there looking all forlorn, Betsy (as is her way) decided to be helpful and said *Well, maybe it would be okay if you played drone chords behind us, like G when we're playing a tune in G, so you can get the feel of how the music goes*. The guy jumped on this and began to drone away, until Brian walked into the back room again, saw him and said *I thought I told you not to play that thing. Out!*

So that was the standard of session etiquette in Nanny O'Brien's, such as it was. But fortunately we were not often subjected to one common session plague, rogue armies of bodhran players, thanks to one of our best drummers, a guy named Rick Rider who strictly enforced the one-drummer-at-a-time rule. Rick had become a master of the idiosyncratic bodhran style of one of Ireland's greats, Tommy Hayes of Stockton's Wing fame, purely by working with an instructional videotape. Never had he met the man or worked with another bodhran teacher, never had he been to Ireland or even to one of the Irish music summer schools like Augusta or Swannanoa, but somehow Rick had absorbed the essence of what drumming is all about in Irish music. Less is more. And somehow Rick was able to impart that ethos in a gentle way to the motley assortment of drummers who would wander into the session, keeping them all in line. And it was indeed a motley bunch. I recall one guy who showed up for a few months with a bongo drum just slightly smaller than a 50-gallon drum. He sat next to me one night, and partly to make conversation but mainly to try to drive home a subtle point I said to him *Gosh, you must get a lot of strange looks walking down Connecticut Avenue with that thing.* His response? *Nah, I have this*, and he pulled out an olive drab duffel bag as big as a body bag. It was nights like that when we all really appreciated having Rick around at the session.

If only we'd had someone like Rick to handle all the guitar, bouzouki, ukulele and mando-banjo offenders. And the mando-banjo guy was the worst, by far. It's not that he lacked musical talent, because he didn't. He just shouldn't have been playing that instrument, and he most certainly shouldn't have been playing Irish music on it. One night he stopped the session craic entirely with a tremolo version of the air *Ar Éireann Ní Neosainn Cé Hí*. Halfway through it, Rob turned to me and whispered *For Tuscany, I'll not tell her name.* Somewhere in Tuscany, they weren't telling his name either. Or if they were, there was an expletive attached.

> *Never was in tune*
> *Rear view mirror on the top*
> *Doc could make it sing*

The typical answer whenever someone asks when the "good old days" of something were is "about six months before you got here." But for the Nanny O'Brien's session, the answer is different. The good old days were when the piano was in the corner in the front end of the back room, with the session surrounding it in an expanding set of semi-circles. Actually, you can trace the steady decline of the session to the day when the piano was moved to the other corner to make room for a built-in corner bench where it used to sit. This meant that instead of being in the center of the session the piano now sat behind us, out of sight. It was only a matter of time until it was out of the room entirely, not to be replaced. The glue that held the session together was gone.

Not that the piano was being played on every set of tunes. Far from it. Although it looked as old and ratty as the player pianos in the bar scenes of old western movies, it wasn't going to play itself. (Although if it ever did, for sure it wouldn't have been in tune.) Marc Glickman would play it, but he wasn't there every week. Doc *was* there every week, but even though he's the son of a bar-room piano player and has been tinkling the ivories himself since a very early age, he would spend more time not playing that piano than he would playing it. He'd have the fiddle out, or he'd be up at the bar getting another pint, or maybe he'd be out with the others checking the air in the tires. But timing is everything, and Doc's timing was impeccable. He always knew when the session was starting to lose focus. Sometimes it was obvious to all of us, like when competing tunes would erupt from the far sides of the room, and neither one would give up because the group was so big that the one side couldn't hear what was being played on the other. Other times it wasn't that cut and dried. But Doc knew when to come into the room, sit down on the bench, cast a glance into the rear view mirror conveniently mounted on top of the piano, and start pounding out the chords. Instantly everyone was back on the same sheet of music. (So to speak, because if anyone actually did show up with a sheet of music at an Irish session they'd be hounded out in disgrace.)

Or late in the evening, around midnight as the tunes began to wind down and you were thinking about packing up and heading home, in would walk Doc, pint in hand, to sit down at the piano. Invariably he'd launch into The Graf Spey in what he always calls the people's key, C major, and the session would be reborn, often to live until closing time of two a.m. I rarely lasted that long myself (the curse of the day job) but I know for a fact that the best music and craic always came out in those late hours. How do I know that? Because I'd hear all about it the next week, and utter a curse *at* the day job. But even today I cannot hear The Graf Spey without immediately thinking of Doc and that piano, and even though I'm a flute player I can only play that tune in C, not D like every other flute player in the world would want to. And if I ever happen to be in a music store where they sell pianos, I wonder why they're not all equipped with a rear view mirror as standard equipment.

*Kathleen's trivia quiz*
*Drew Hillman, Jim Curtin too*
*Sadly are long gone*

In the hospitality business – which is the category where pub ownership falls, even though any drunk ever tossed to the curb by a bouncer would dispute that – Monday night is the slow night of the week and thus the regular staff's night off. At Nanny O'Brien's this meant that Brian Gaffney's wife Kathleen would be working the back room instead of minding the store at home like she did the rest of the week. Kathleen loved the session – although in retrospect I do wonder why, because so many of us were drinking the two free pints without bothering to tip for them – and one of her, and our, favorite parts of the evening was when she'd step into the back room, wait for the music to stop, and declare *Trivia question for the free pint of Guinness!* Usually the question had something to do with Irish history or geography, U2, stuff like that, and whoever yelled out the correct answer first got the pint. Anyone in the room could win, not just a musician, and every once in a while I did. But there was this one time that my win came as easy as taking candy from a baby. Someone up front had talked Kathleen into doing a joke question, so she came into the back and yelled out *How long was Brian Boru's penis?* An uncomfortable silence descended on the room, so quiet you could hear a pin drop, and it seemed to go on for an eternity – until I decided to venture an answer. I said *Nine inches* and she immediately thrust the pint into my hand, turned around and hustled out of the room. After that my standard answer to the trivia question, whatever it was, was always *Nine inches.* I never won again, but I usually got a smile out of Kathleen.

*Always comes in late*
*Out checking air in the tires*
*Tell me, do you sing?*

One thing I noticed even while I was still the newbie stuck sitting in the back at the Monday night session was that after a few long blasts of tunes many of the players sitting up front would get up and disappear from the room, usually heading out the back door into the alley behind the pub where they had parked. Their prime seats remained empty while the rest of us struggled on, and then after a while they'd return and start up a new blast of tunes. Sometimes after their hiatus they'd repeat the tunes ten or even twenty times before changing to the next one, instead of the usual three. I thought they were just doing us newbies a favor by playing them longer so we'd have more time to learn them. The session mood would become very mellow around that time, too, which I rather liked. After seeing this scenario play out a few times I asked where they were all going, and was told that they were checking the air in the tires. I gave silent thanks that my own tires were still fairly new, had good tread on them and didn't leak, because I was sure no one would save my seat, lousy as it was, if I had to leave in mid-session to walk the several blocks to where I was parked in order to make sure I wasn't getting a flat. I figured that was just another thing that separated me from the real musicians. Real musicians don't have good tires.

A couple of years later I was glad that I had good tires, though. I got laid off from my day job and discovered that since the last time I'd gone job hunting all the companies had decided that they would only hire people who had good tires. In fact, they even had a test where they took a sample of your bodily fluids to make sure that you hadn't been checking the air in your tires recently. And then after I got that job I had to get a government security clearance and I found out that our national security is *incredibly* dependent on having good tires. I never would have known! In fact, the lady who did my security investigation was aghast to discover that I knew and hung around with people who needed to check the air in their tires. I said *Sorry, I play music so a lot of my friends are musicians. Everyone knows real musicians don't have good tires.* Some day, if the economy quits tanking, maybe I can retire and just play music. Then I can be the only one worrying if I need to check the air in my tires or not.

Good tires or no, it was the rare visitor to the session who managed to escape the query from Doc. *Do you sing?* The question was purely rhetorical (at least that's how I always interpreted it whenever *I* was asked) but occasionally it elicited a positive response – although rare was the time that the resultant singing turned out to be a positive experience. The real singers know who they are, and they know they don't need to be asked in order to sing. But they also know that if ever they *are* asked to sing, it needs to be more than once before a song will come forth from them. Three times is usually about right. *Tell me, do you sing? Ah, no, I couldn't. Oh come on, now, give us a song. Ah, no, no. Maybe tomorrow. Quieten down now, folks. Shhh. Your man has a song for us, does he not? Ah well, if you insist....* A good song is always worth the effort it takes to get it out.

Then there was the time that the great Kerry box player Johnny O'Leary was doing some gigs nearby, and his handler on the U.S. end decided that he needed to be brought to the Nanny's session the very same day he got off the flight at Dulles, or maybe it was BWI. Anyway, between the jet lag and his thick Kerry accent we were only able to make out about one of every three words he said. That didn't stop Doc from asking the question. *Tell me Mr. O'Leary, do you sing?* He didn't, but I don't know if that was because he really didn't sing or he just didn't understand the question.

*Kids' session tonight*
*Pitchers, glasses everywhere*
*"Dum Dum" at the end*

Even after I had worked my way up the session ladder to a point where I could legitimately command a seat in the front circle of players, I would still try to get to Nanny's as early as possible to be sure of snagging a good seat. The circle at the session wasn't really a circle, it was more of a box since we were seated in a corner around two or three square tables that had been pushed together to make a long rectangle. As a flute player it's good to have a wall somewhere in front of you to bounce your sound back so you can hear what you're playing, and I always tried to get there early enough to claim a seat where I'd be shooting my sound straight into the corner. But once a month my real-estate grab was thwarted by a bunch of kids. I could never keep track of when it was scheduled, so I'd walk into Nanny's shortly after eight p.m. expecting the pub to be empty and find the back room absolutely packed, with people spilling out into the front room. The normal convention of keeping a small pathway through the crowd so a drinker from the front could get to the jacks in the back was clearly suspended, but it didn't matter because all the drinkers were in the back. And they were drinking Coke. Karen Ashbrook – one of the world's best players of one of the most-maligned instruments in Irish music, the hammered dulcimer – was again doing penance for her sin by running a kids' session in the bar before the big boys came in to play.

I always thought Karen was Jewish, until she told me a few years ago she's not. Maybe I thought that because she plays Klezmer music along with the Irish, or maybe because I've met so many other Jewish folks who play Irish music. Myron, Orion, Danny too, I think. But whatever her heritage, Karen has been downright rabbinical in her zeal to bring young players into Irish music. The monthly kids' session was their recital, an opportunity to play in a public setting, with no pressure other than to try to drink as many pitchers of free Coke in one hour as is humanly possible. Most if not all of the kids were too young to drive themselves there, so their parents were along for the evening. But as best I could tell, none of them were "stage parents" forcing their kids into coming. The parents were there because the kids wanted to be there. And for some of them, they were also there to carry the instrument – like for the harp players, whose instrument case could double as a second home for the kid if the family ever got evicted from their real house.

There were usually as many kids at the kids' session as there were players at the "real" session that followed it, as soon as Kathleen was able to get in there and clean all the spilled Coke off the tables so we could observe the changing of the guard. And a few of those kids who played at that session would soon begin hanging around for the regular session, putting the rest of us to shame before long. I think here of Lily Smigen-Rothkopf the harp player, who went off to university in Limerick and is now touring the world playing innovative yet tradition-based music as Lily Neill. I hope in a few years when she's truly famous she'll still be talking about playing together with us at Nanny O'Brien's, like she does now. Knowing her and knowing where she came from, I've no doubt she will.

With as many tunes as there are in Irish music, it's amazing how few there are that I actually don't like. A couple remain from my dancing days, like the Sweets of May and the High Cauld Cap, but those are somewhat tainted by their association with particular dances I never liked either. But one tune I have always absolutely despised is a polka called John Ryan's. It doesn't have the nickname Dum Dum for nothing. But whenever that unfortunate tune becomes an earworm for me, its nastiness is always tempered by the memory that it was the closing tune played every month at the kids' session at Nanny's, right before Kathleen would come in to wipe up. I'm sure all those kids carry that same association for the tune around with them, and it's a sign of their superior upbringing that none of them has yet included it on any CD they've released. If ever I record a CD, I won't either!

*Brendan Mulvihill*
*Eileen Ivers, Martin Hayes*
*Not seen oft enough*

If there was one eternal truth about Nanny O'Brien's, it's what Brian Gaffney always said. You never knew who was going to walk in – and that wasn't just on session night, either. For many years, Brendan Mulvihill was the regular Wednesday night entertainment in the pub, playing with Brian on the small stage in the front room. Although you did actually know that Brendan would be walking into Nanny's that night, there was always the question of when. But whenever he did, you knew the fiddling would be magical. Brendan always had a special place in Nanny O'Brien's. Even though he lived many miles away and didn't drive, Nanny's was practically his local. He could walk in anytime. Perhaps that was the knowledge that spread through the worldwide community of Irish musicians and made Nanny's a destination spot for them whenever they'd happen to be in Washington. Or perhaps it was Brian's willingness to turn his pub into a gig venue for touring musicians to fill what would otherwise have been an off night in their calendars with the chance to pick up a few extra bucks. It couldn't have been much, since the place was small and I doubt everyone who was there on gig nights was paying the ten or fifteen buck cover charge. I'm sure the nonstop dart throwers in the back weren't, and I sure hope all those folks at the end of the bar who talked all through the evening and never paid attention to a note of the music weren't either – although it was always the thought that they might actually have been paying customers that kept me from asking them to shut up. That and the fact I knew they never would, of course.

There were some memorable concert nights at Nanny's. Josephine Marsh. Seamus Begley and a barefoot, dreadlocked Stephen Cooney – *in the middle of winter*. Andy M. Stewart and Gerry O'Beirne. Moving Cloud – Kevin Crawford, Paul Brock, Maeve Donnelly, Manus McGuire, with Carl Hession *and* his keyboard all up on the postage-stamp stage. The two Pauls, McGrattan and O'Shaughnessy. Frankie Gavin. Niall and Cillian Vallely. But the one night that sticks with me the most was when Tommy Peoples played Nanny's, the second time. The first one had been quite the event, mind you. Brian sold so many advance tickets for that one that he had to set up a dozen or so auxiliary tables to seat the crowd, and he was for once able to shut down the dart throwers and silence all the overly chatty punters – entirely befitting the first Washington visit in living memory of one of Irish music's true icons. By the time of Tommy's second visit to Nanny's a year or two later, much of the hype had died down but there was still a good crowd, including nearly all of the Monday night session regulars. And then during the break, Brian's saying proved true yet again as Matt Molloy, in town with The Chieftains, came walking in the door. A third chair was placed on stage where Tommy had played the first half of the concert with Brian Gaffney on guitar, and we in the audience were soon treated to a live rendition of much of the seminal Molloy/Brady/Peoples album, with Brian playing the Paul Brady role. That album had always been one of the prime – if not *the* prime – feeder albums for the session, so it was a treat beyond belief for us to sit at the bar a mere five or ten feet away and see and hear it live. At one point they started off on a set of tunes and said *Wait, haven't we played that one already?* To which our response was *Who cares? Play it again. Play them all again!*

There was often a session after these Nanny's concert nights, but I don't think I ever stayed for one because they were invariably slow to get started and I always had the next morning's alarm staring me in the face. But if ever word came around that there might be someone special popping in that week for the Monday session, I was always there even earlier than usual to get a seat and prepared to stay for the duration. When *Riverdance* was in town for its two-week run at Wolf Trap, the cast made Nanny's its after-performance watering hole for the duration of the run. But Monday night was the one night they were dark, so everyone *knew* they'd be there for the session. Eileen Ivers was front and center in the session circle – she may have been playing the blue fiddle, I don't really remember, but alas she wasn't wearing the purple velvet Doc Martens she featured on stage – but the Riverdance musician I remember most from that night was the box player sitting in the back with a comely young lass on his lap and the accordion on her lap as he played the night away with his arms around her. Sadly, I knew right then and there that all the practice in the world would never get *me* to that point. Yet I'm still playing today. I guess I must really like the music.

The glory days of Nanny O'Brien's largely overlapped the best years of the Washington Irish Folk Festival, and this ensured that there would always be one or two festival performers who wanted to hang around a while after the festival – or who overslept and missed their flight home – and would come to Nanny's on the Monday night for some tunes and craic. Why Irish musicians will travel the world over and always end up in the Irish pub in town instead of sampling the local flavor has been something that's always eluded me. But many's the time it did wonders for our session evening, so I'm not complaining. The Tulla Ceili Band was touring in 1997 in support of its fiftieth anniversary CD and they made the trip to Nanny's the day after they played the festival at Wolf Trap, basically taking over the session for the night with the rest of us along for the ride. The room was packed so full that Tina was sitting on top of the cigarette machine in the back, playing along on her flute. The great Martin Hayes, a man who will never be able to change his hairstyle because it has truly come to identify him – and boy, I bet he's glad he doesn't have Donald Trump's hair – was there that night with the band his father started 50 years before. But as august and imposing a presence as Martin is whenever and wherever Irish music is played, it was old P.J. Hayes who ran the show that night. Only a few years short of his death from Parkinson's disease, he really couldn't play the fiddle any more although you'd have to be sitting right next to him to know it because he still would finger the notes and move the bow. But with a glance or a quiet word from him the other members of the band knew exactly what tune would be played next, and the look in his eyes after the set was done would tell them and us that it had been played well. We all left that night basking in the glow of a great session. I'd like to think the members of the Tulla Band felt the same way.

The great Dublin singer Frank Harte was my first and longest-lasting touchstone into the totality of the Irish tradition of music, song and dance. Three branches from the same root that have each grown strong, but largely apart. Frank talked often of the gulf that seems to exist between music and song and his hopes that it might some day be bridged. Dancers and musicians might *try* to inhabit different worlds, but since you can't really have dance without music – at least for very long, anyway – they do need to meet eventually. Usually that happens at the ceili, but if there's floor space available there's always a welcome for dancers at the session. But the divide between instrumentalists and singers is sharp, and it particularly comes to bear at the session. Protocol has it that when a song is started the whole pub is shushed so as to give the song its due, which immediately puts everyone else in the room – be they musicians who came to play or punters who came for the craic – out of business for the duration. It takes a strong singer to overcome the resentment that inevitably will follow, and the many suspect singers who try and fail to mount that hurdle only make the task facing the good singer that much more difficult.

On Labor Day weekend in 1998, Frank Harte came to Washington to perform at what was the 22nd annual Irish Folk Festival, held at the Montgomery County Fairgrounds in Gaithersburg. Following the traditional pattern, on the Monday night after the festival there was a great session in Nanny's. It was a truly mad night. The great (and certifiably insane) Kerry box player Brendan Begley was there, leading the frolics, and at one point he and Mick Mulkerrin went mano a mano, face to face in a sean-nós stepdancing challenge, with Brendan stepping and playing the box simultaneously. It was macho and homo-erotic all at once. As the tunes raged madly through the packed room all evening, there in the corner sat Frank, basking in it all. At just the right moment several times during the night, he would burst into a song, quieting the pub instantly. I think there he got to see his ideal session unfold, if just for one night. And if you were to ask me, that would be the greatest night of music that ever happened in Nanny O'Brien's.

If only there had been more nights like that, or at least nights approaching that. For a long time there at least was the expectation that on any given Monday something magical might happen at Nanny's, so no matter how tired you were after a day at work you'd better go, because you could be kicking yourself later if you didn't. Perhaps Nigel Stevens, a great singer and guitarist from the U.K., might make the trip in from his home out past Dulles Airport. Or maybe there'd be some unsung but brilliant player from Ireland who happened to be living in the area or just passing through for a while, like the young fiddler from Laois, Trish Dooley. (But be prepared to play Lads of Laois and Kilty Town at warp speed if that's the case.) At the very least you knew that a major chunk of the area's best players would be there, because if you were looking for a session Nanny's was the only game in town. And good Irish musicians are always looking for a session, if for no other reason than it's not good to be drinking alone.

But then it all changed. Other sessions started popping up as new Irish pubs opened around town. (Thank you, Riverdance.) Most all of these pubs had some Irish connection that could be traced, like Irish investors or Irish owners or fresh-off-the-boat Irish staff or Irish accoutrements. Some of them were built out from floor to ceiling with authentic pieces of Irish pubs brought over and re-assembled here, and others were just tricked out to look "Irish." But whether they were made of the real thing or were just plastic pubs, they still felt fake to me. You can't create an Irish pub overnight, hard as you might try. That's what made places like Nanny O'Brien's so special – they were the real thing. So, in an attempt to be more real, these new pubs wanted music, and to mix things up they often wanted to include a session night in the mix along with the typical ballad singers – especially since the local cadre of guys who can stand up on stage and sing until two a.m. night after night was getting spread thin with all these new pubs opening up. But it's impossible to "fake" a session. You can't just throw up a sign in the window saying "Session Tonight" and expect musicians to show up. So the new pubs started hiring a couple of the better musicians to come and play their session every week, in order to guarantee that there would actually *be* a session on the night they advertised one. This was a new phenomenon in Washington, actually getting paid to play a session, and no musician in his right mind would pass up an opportunity like that. Some of the more enterprising of the local players, guys like Dennis Botzer and Philippe Varlet, were even able to go to these new pubs and talk them into having sessions with themselves as the paid hosts. And for guys like me who were just looking for a place to play where we knew the music would be good, it became easy to go to one of the sessions where we knew who would be playing there that night instead of going to Nanny's like we had been doing for years. So the new sessions began to thrive, while the venerable Nanny O'Brien's session became the home of all manner of non-musical castoffs, the kind of people your mother or Barry Foy's *Field Guide* always warned you about.

Philippe Varlet and Rob Greenway started a Sunday afternoon session in the midst of the great Y2K panic of late 1999 that managed to hang on for nearly a decade at a series of venues. The music was usually mighty at those sessions, often better than the heyday of Nanny's. But the craic was never quite as good. The pub where that session started was perhaps the weirdest place I've ever played in. It was opened by two lesbians (not that there's anything wrong with that, as they said on Seinfeld) and the Irish connection was that one of them, who happened to be black, had played professional basketball in Ireland. (Who knew there was even hoops at all in Ireland, much less pro?) The pub was on the second story of a strip building in Silver Spring, and even after being decked out in its full Irish raiment it still had all the ambience of a Kinko's. Indeed it may have been a Kinko's in a previous life, because it had an air conditioning system worthy of a computer server room. I started a set of tunes there once, only to be met by strange looks from everyone else in the circle. I thought for sure I was seriously out of tune or making a complete bollocks of the tunes, but it turned out that they were all staring at me because it was so cold in there that every time I hit a D on the flute, thereby closing all the holes, a little puff of steam was coming out the end!

The session soldiered on there for about a year, in a bar devoid of patrons, until football season rolled around and the management decided to cancel it and re-image the pub as a sports bar. But apparently the masses didn't cotton to watching the Redskins lose in a Kinko's, or maybe it was that people preferred to eat greasy fried things in a place where they occasionally (or at least once) cleaned the grease traps. Whatever the reason, shortly after we quit playing there the pub went out of business. The session moved on to some other interim stops, including a barbecue joint in Silver Spring and even Nanny O'Brien's for a while, before settling in at a new pub near the Pentagon called Sin E. *Sin e* is Irish for "that's it", but for the session it eventually became clear that Sin E wasn't it. They had no clue at all what a session was supposed to be. The manager's comment to Philippe shortly before he gave the boot to the session says it all. *You guys have been practicing for two years* he said. *When are you going to start playing?* Heh. I walk through that mall from time to time to do a bit of shopping, and every time I do Sin E is still there, as plastic as ever. They can practice all they want, they'll never be a real Irish pub.

Philippe's car was barely out of the parking garage under Sin E before he was on the phone swinging a deal to move the Sunday session to a new pub in Bethesda called Ri Ra that had actually just finished booking him and Rob to do a Wednesday night session. If you can believe the highfaluting mission statement on their website, *Rí Rá comes from "Rí Rá agus Ruaile Buaile", a phrase translating roughly as divilment, good fun or any sociable activity that improves with fine food, a nice pint of Guinness or dram of Uisce Beatha (whiskey).* Although most of their staff was never on board with it, for six or seven years the session found a home twice a week at Ri Ra. Some good music was made there, but I'm hard pressed to recall any divilment. Perhaps that has to do with the clientele of that establishment, such as the family that was sitting in the booth next to us one Sunday afternoon. Normally I don't pay much notice to the punters at a session (comely young maidens excepted) but something about those two blond-headed kids looked familiar. So my eyes shifted first to the mother – again she looked familiar – and then to the father. Aha! It was the recently sworn-in Chief Justice of the Supreme Court John Roberts, who had been pictured at the time of his nomination with the wife and kids in a tableau straight out of the 1950s – which is by coincidence the same place his values come from. I don't know what kind of impression we scruffy musicians made on him, but we certainly didn't see an upsurge in crowd size after his visit. Although it would be hard to tell, really, as right wing conservatives don't tend to be much into divilment – unless they're trying to suppress it, that is.

But I do have to give the Republicans one thing – they tip well. Not that we had a tip jar out at the session, mind you. In fact I don't think I've ever seen a tip jar at a traditional music session. Session leaders and players, if they're getting paid at all, are making less than a Starbucks barista. But we do have our pride. Still, that doesn't stop listeners from dropping a bill on the session table as they walk out every now and then. Usually it's a five or a ten, which always makes me wonder how they expect seven or eight musicians to divvy it up at the end of the night. Usually we just put it toward the bar tab (yes, very often already-underpaid musicians are forced to pay for their own drink at sessions) or add it to the waiter's tip. One cold January night at RiRa, though, a youngster came up to the table and dropped a bill on us, saying *My father told me to give you this. Thanks for the music.* Thinking it was the usual fiver, we mumbled *Hey, you're welcome* and played on. An hour or so later, one of us picked up the bill and we were amazed to discover it was a C note. It seems the generous punter was in town for George W. Bush's inauguration the next day. Clearly he was unaware of the political persuasion of the musicians who were playing for him that night, or maybe he'd have thought twice about that tip!

Mr. Chief Justice Roberts gave us a nice tip, too, although he waited several years to deliver it. When the Obamacare bill came before the Court for review, to the surprise of everyone the Chief Justice voted counter to his conservative colleagues in favor of it. A few months after that, he was outed by *Newsweek* magazine as being a closet Irish dancer. Seems his wife is the daughter of Irish immigrants and they own a small vacation cottage near her mother's home townland. *Newsweek* even described him as a "raucous Irish dancer" and said Irish ceili or set dancing is how he unwinds from his hectic schedule at the court. When I read that, I wondered where it was that he does his unwinding via Irish dance, since to my knowledge he's never been seen at a session or ceili in Washington other than that time at RiRa. Then I read further into the article and saw that he's been a few times to the very same Willie Clancy Week where I first learned Irish set dancing from Joe and Siobhan O'Donovan. I guess what they say is true. What happens in Miltown stays in Miltown.

If you've been paying attention so far, it will come as no surprise that the most enterprising person around in searching out new venues for a session is one Dennis "Doc" Botzer. Casting their net far and wide, Doc and his banjo-playing neighbor Patrick Cavanagh started a session at a pub called Sean Donlon's in Annapolis, some 35 miles from the street in Silver Spring where they lived a block apart. They would carpool there every Tuesday night to sit next to each other and play tunes, and when I got laid off from my day job in 2001 I started driving the 45 miles from my own house to join them. Even after I found work, I kept going there because the Nanny's session had deteriorated so much. The lust for tunes will make normally sane people do crazy things like that. Doc and Patrick were at least getting paid the session-host pittance; I wasn't. But it was almost always a good session and worth the long drive and midweek late night. One summer Tuesday I talked my neighbors Betsy and Orion into going to Annapolis with me for the session. Doc, Patrick, Spencer, Josh and I took our usual places up on the stage in the bar's front window, but there wasn't room for Betsy and Orion so they had to take seats on chairs below the stage, facing us. Not that bad a setup, since the stage was only a few feet tall. But being up there did give us boyos a nice view of the action out in the pub, which was usually filled with midshipmen from the nearby Naval Academy. This particular evening they were apparently conducting training exercises for future Tailhook operations, and they were joined in their drunken revelry by some of Annapolis's finest young women. At one point, one of these ladies hopped up onto the bar to work on her pole-dancing moves. Apparently she was drunk enough that the lack of a pole didn't matter, and she proved quite flexible and fetching up there even though she did forget that she was supposed to be removing pieces of clothing as part of the dance. Ah, well, you can't have everything. It was at that precise moment that Betsy, who couldn't see what was happening behind her back, decided to start a new set of tunes. She was quite miffed that no one would join in with her, even as she made it well into the first tune. What she didn't realize, though, is that it's hard to play Irish music while you're drooling. Even if you don't play the flute.

Unfortunately Sean Donlon and the missus had a small disagreement on the value of having a session in their pub, and as is always the way of the world the woman of the house won out. We came in from the cold one midwinter Tuesday night to find ourselves frozen out. No problem. Doc got on the horn to Castlebay, only a few blocks away, and we soon found ourselves taking a quick hike through Annapolis, instruments and all, to set up shop there. That lasted a year or so until we were told to hit the road again. But this time, a new pub called McGinty's had opened up right in downtown Silver Spring and Doc and Patrick were able to trade an hour or more of driving for more time playing tunes and drinking pints. Sounds like a good trade-off, huh? And it is, but not often enough for me. Who would believe that it can take as long or even longer to drive the 21 miles from my house to Silver Spring as it does to drive the 45 miles to Annapolis? Answer: those hundreds of thousands of my neighbors who have taken the rush out of – and put about five extra hours into – what used to be rush hour. The folks who run McGinty's must have sensed my pain, because a year or so later they opened a southern outpost much closer to my house, and Brendan Bell, Josh Dukes and Danny Noveck started a session there. We all found it much easier to get to than other session pubs, but unfortunately no one else did – particularly punters. Management was on top of that situation, though, and poised to implement a solution on their very first St. Patrick's Day, a holiday that is to Irish pubs as Christmas is to the retail industry – namely a single golden day whose income can alleviate all economic sins committed during the rest of the year.

I was booked to play at lunchtime on that Paddy's Day, and allowed to invite another musician of my choosing to play with me. My choices were limited, thanks to the McGinty's folks not offering me the gig until a week beforehand. Everyone I knew already had a gig, except for my young friend Kelly, a whiz on the pipes, flute and fiddle. So I texted her to see if she wanted the gig. Her reply? *Well, I'd have to cut class to do it, so…sure!* Kelly clearly has her priorities in order. We arrived shortly before noon on the 17th, with me a little apprehensive about having to play without a sound system in front of what I expected would be a rowdy crowd. At most Irish pubs, they open the doors at dawn on Paddy's Day and by noon there's a line out the door like an Apple store on iPhone launch day – with the big difference being that the crowd inside an Apple store is sober. Kelly and I were ushered to a prime table right by the front window in a room that had about three tables occupied by folks eating lunch. At the crack of noon we launched into our first set of tunes, and when we were done the manager approached us. *Um, we've had a few complaints that the music is too loud. We're going to move you into the back by the bar.* As we were relocating, I said to Kelly *Who comes to an Irish pub on St. Patrick's Day for a little peace and quiet?!?!?* We played in a nook by the bar for the next three hours, joined after a while by our friends Orion on fiddle and Lori on flute, and had no further complaints. Perhaps that had something to do with there being no one in the pub by the time we were done – save for the staff, one of whom issued us our checks, and we were off. Less than a year later, the pub closed, which of course led to the demise of the session. Not only that, no other pub has offered me a gig since that Paddy's Day in McGinty's. Surely there's no correlation?

I first walked into Nanny O'Brien's those many years ago with much to learn. And as the years have passed, I have learned a lot – some of it expected, some not. I hoped and expected to learn what it takes to become a session player, and I'm happy now to know that I was up to the task. I've learned more than enough to be able to run an Irish pub myself, but also know that I'm nowhere near crazy enough to do that. And I've been surprised to learn how resilient the session community is, and the lengths to which they'll go to keep the session going. Why, shortly after the McGinty's session ended because the pub went belly-up, those same owners opened up a new bar in what looks to be a better location. Doc went to them with an offer they couldn't refuse. He gave them a piano on the condition that he could host a weekly session around it. So far, it's working. Then he did the same thing at the other McGinty's up in Silver Spring. Now I'm afraid to invite Doc over for a tune at my house. He might drop a piano on me, and I have nowhere to put it.

The biggest thing I've learned, though, is that while the session is all about the music it's even more about community. I've seen sessions in the area spread out to other venues and other days, as either a cause or an effect of the decline of the session at Nanny's. I've seen new sessions start up and thrive for years, while others have begun and perished in just a matter of weeks. I've seen that no matter how much a pub owner says he likes and wants a session when it starts, inevitably he'll get tired of it and cancel it in favor of showing football games on massive television screens. (Apparently pub owners find it easier to deal with keeping track of the remote than to appreciate the quirks of musicians, even though the annual payment for the TV hardware and license has to dwarf the paltry sums paid to real live musicians.) I've seen that for traditional musicians, hope (or the quest for a free pint) springs eternal, and that every time one session dies another one or two or three soon springs up somewhere else. It feels now like there are more sessions around me than ever, and indeed there are. But as was said when cable TV was new ("500 channels and there's nothing on") even with all these sessions going on it often feels like there's nowhere to play. There's no focus to the scene like there was in the heyday of Nanny O'Brien's. Music and memories are still being made, but it's just not the same any more. And that's a bit sad.

# The Tradition

The year 1985 was a big one for me, and also a momentous time for Irish traditional music. That's because, after a couple of years messing around with the music in the privacy of my living room, it's when I made my big burst onto the scene. That is, if you define "bursting onto the scene" as going to the Irish Festival at Glen Echo Park for the first time and then later that summer, armed with guitar (!) and hammered dulcimer (?), going on vacation to the Irish Week at Augusta. So it's been over a quarter of a century that I have been obsessed with this music, and I guess I'm a bit of an old-timer on the scene now. You might even think I got here early, which perhaps I did. But if in fact I was early, I was not early enough to have seen The Irish Tradition in their heyday.

My earliest memories of entering this new world of Irish music include the realization that there were two bands whose presence permeated the scene in Washington, indeed defining it. They were Celtic Thunder and The Irish Tradition, both of whom had come south from the rich Irish American culture of New York City. Celtic Thunder I could see every month, since they were the regular band at the ceilis where I went to dance the new steps and figures I was learning. But all I knew of The Irish Tradition – Brendan Mulvihill, Billy McComiskey and Andy O'Brien – I heard first by word of mouth and later by getting my hands on a couple of their recordings. Brendan, Billy and Andy came down to Washington from New York in 1975 or 1976 for what was supposed to have been a one-week gig at The Dubliner on Capitol Hill. But they were such a hit that the week ended up stretching into several years, years when they basically put Irish music on the map in the Nation's Capital. In a city which then had little discernible Irish ethnic presence – a couple of Irish bars and a bit of ceili dancing here and there – this group suddenly and unexpectedly became one of the hottest tickets in town. Trendiness may have been the spark that ignited their ride, but its extended run was surely fueled by nothing other than sheer virtuosity and talent, as anyone who's ever heard Andy sing or Brendan or Billy play can attest.

But then, after several years and three albums, the Tradition disbanded, leaving it for the old-timers on the scene to recall for newbies like me the magical sense of levity, lunacy and downright mayhem that had trailed their marvelous musical machine around like drops of leaking oil. The stories I heard were legion, and are aptly summed up in the title of the Tradition's final recording, "The Times We've Had." After hearing those tales, I was really not surprised that the band was no more. I've never been married (came close once, but that's another story) and I've never been in a band, but even I know that the only thing harder than keeping a marriage together is keeping a band together. And the more the fun and the higher the times in a marriage or a band, often the harder it becomes to keep it going. Brendan, Billy and Andy each ended up moving to Baltimore at some point along the way (although Brendan is back in DC now), and Andy O'Brien had pretty much faded into obscurity by the time I came on the scene. But Brendan and Billy, by virtue of their mere presence, continued to exert enormous influence on the music and dancing in Washington. I eventually met them both, and learned that they had not actually played together since the Tradition broke up. I never knew (or asked) why. They were civil enough with each other when they ended up in the same place, so I figured that whatever rift there was between them was one of those "artistic differences" things, and left it at that.

Brendan was making great music with Donna Long, and there was no one better for playing for the dancers than Billy. And so it remained for almost the entire first decade I was on the scene. (Although now I do remember there was one notable crack in the musical ice between Brendan and Billy – at Augusta in the early '90s when they both sat down with Mick Moloney and Eugene O'Donnell in one of the lunchtime concerts for a memorable rendition of Loftus Jones, one of their staples in the Tradition. I still have a tape of that somewhere...)

Then, sometime around 1993, an Irish fellow called Noel Coyne emerged on the scene. Actually, he re-emerged, because although I'd not met him he had apparently been ubiquitous around here in the heyday of the Tradition, since all of the (then) old-timers knew him. He didn't play or dance himself, but he loved the music. And, in the great tradition of Irishmen, he was a grand schemer, full of energy. He had lots of ideas, which in the time-honored tradition of grand Irish schemers never came to fruition. Except that one of his grand schemes actually did – a reunion of The Irish Tradition. When I first met him, all Noel had was the idea. He was convinced he could talk Brendan, Billy and Andy into playing together again, if only an occasion grand enough for that to happen could occur. He approached first Mike Denney and then the whole of the Greater Washington Ceili Club Board with his proposal: Produce a grand dinner-dance in the Christmas holiday season at which the reunion of The Irish Tradition would be the featured attraction. The GWCC was not then in the dinner-dance business, unless you counted our monthly ceili that featured a potluck supper during the break. But Noel's sights were set much higher than that. He wanted a high-priced catered affair.

Somehow the board bought off on his proposal. I don't recall how that happened, although I'm sure there was the usual financial trepidation. Our coffers must have been relatively flush at the time, or maybe we pre-conditioned the whole thing on there being enough advance ticket sales before we'd make an irrevocable financial commitment. Normally you don't like to do that kind of thing, booking bands for an evening and then yanking the rug out from under them before the gig has a chance to be played. But we were justifiably worried that a band that hadn't played together for years might get cold feet and bail out on *us*, so perhaps turnabout was fair play there. But whatever it took to get the wheels rolling, it happened. A Knights of Columbus hall in Arlington was booked, a menu featuring Cornish game hens and bottles of white wine was ordered up from a caterer, and I set to work making posters and flyers on my recently acquired first personal computer, a Gateway 2000. (Those were indeed innocent times, when a computer could safely be named after the upcoming new millennium because the massive Y2K scare was not yet even a gleam in the fearmonger's eye.) I spent dozens of hours pushing that computer's primitive capabilities to their limit to produce a two-color poster with scanned stock images of an accordion, a guitar and a fiddle that was suitable for printing on large stock at my neighborhood Kinko's. Wendy Newton, whose Green Linnet label released all the Tradition's albums, was using the money she should have been paying her artists as royalties to instead throw an "Irish Music Weekend Party of the Year" at a Jewish resort in the Catskills a month or two before our event, so I went there and plastered the place with posters. I seriously doubt that even one person came to the dinner-dance on account of those posters (several may in fact have been scared away) but that whole exercise did give me an appreciation for what graphic designers go through every single day. Thinking back on it also makes me realize how far computers have come since then. A first grader armed with an iPhone today could make a better-looking poster than I did then!

As the day approached it became increasingly apparent that we'd sell enough tickets to make the event a financial success. More importantly, our confidence increased that the Tradition would actually show up and play together. At last, on a chilly Friday evening in early December 1994, the old-timers had the chance to re-live their halcyon days, while myself and many other newcomers were able to get a first-hand glimpse of what all the fuss had been about. The otherwise nondescript K of C hall had been decorated for the season with holly centerpieces at each table that were hand-made by Trish Callahan, with lots of flowers and apples and such tacked onto them. With the Cornish game hens and white wine on the menu in place of Guinness and simple pub fare, the venue was a bit – make that a good bit – more upscale than some of the places where the Tradition had made their mark years before. Along with the persistent buzz of anticipation preceding the event there had been a fair bit of apprehension on the part of performers and audience alike as to whether the trio would be able to recapture the magical musical rapport they'd once shared, the elusive *je ne sais quoi* which had once made it all seem so natural and so right. But it didn't take long after the three lads struck up their first notes for any remaining apprehensions to fade away like so many drops of morning dew, and it wasn't long thereafter that any pretenses of formality about the occasion were dropped altogether.

Wendy Newton was there that night – not to write any royalty checks, but to do lots of bragging about how the trio's successes in the '70s and '80s had put her record label on the map and thereby changed her life. Before the first set of tunes even ended, Wendy and Marleen

Denney pulled the carefully decorated and arranged dinner tables across the thirty foot moat between them and the stage so that they were right up close. Requests for old favorites were soon being yelled out from the audience or scribbled on napkins and tossed up on stage. It was as if the entire assembly had been shipped back in time to the tiny front room of The Dubliner, circa 1978 or so, with the only difference being the increased musical maturity brought to Brendan and Billy's always inspired playing and the extra wallop of mellowness added to Andy's ever-smooth voice by the intervening years. As the performance came to a close, pieces of Trish Callahan's carefully hand-crafted holly centerpieces came flying up on stage in tribute, with Wendy, Marleen and Mike Denney leading the charge. If sequels are never as good as the original, I shudder to think what it must have been like and how good it must have been to see The Irish Tradition back in the day, when they were the toast of Washington. Perhaps that had something to do with the perfectly coiffed heads of prematurely grey hair Mike Denney and Wendy Newton were sporting that night.

But, as it's often said, you can't go home again. Although flushed with the success of that brilliant night in December, the three members of The Irish Tradition agreed after it was over that they wouldn't be going back to work again as a full-time group. But having discovered the old magic still hovering out there within their reach, they didn't want to let it escape completely again into faded memory. So they did come back together again on occasion to perform as The Irish Tradition. The first time was at the next spring's Wolf Trap Irish Festival (it rained), and there were a few more times after that. I remember once on a Labor Day weekend at Nanny O'Brien's, and they may have done the festival again once or twice before it folded in Y2K. But Andy O'Brien has once gain faded into obscurity (the last time I remember seeing him was a couple of years ago when he showed up to hear Liz Carroll at Jammin' Java and was coaxed into a song), and while Brendan and Billy do continue to play together now and then, it's typically with Zan McLeod – sort of a Tradition Lite, because Zan doesn't sing. But most of the time, Billy is the Musical Mayor of Baltimore and Brendan does the all-too-rare solo gigs around DC.

So now here it is fifteen years later. The grand schemer Noel Coyne has long since moved away, to Colorado I think, where his wife got a nice new job. Mike and Marleen Denney moved up to Maine a few years ago, I hear. There are probably not many people still on the scene today who heard the Tradition at their reunion gig, much less in their original incarnation. Wendy Newton was never forced to pay royalties, but a lawsuit filed by some of the more disgruntled musicians in her stable of artists did force her to sell her Green Linnet label to Compass Records, who are at least keeping the old Irish Tradition albums in print. Hopefully they are paying royalties now too, but I wouldn't count on it.

One last post-script to that Tradition reunion evening: From my earliest days on the scene I have been known as the guy who bakes the giant cookies. First I brought them as my contribution to the potluck dinners at GWCC ceilis, then I started bringing them to tune parties in the hope that if my flute-playing prowess didn't earn me repeat invitations my cookies might. I've got many different kinds that I make, and lately I've been branching out into other sweets like cupcakes, mini-tarts, truffles and the like. But in all the years of baking, there has only been one time that someone has asked if they could pay me to make some cookies for them. It was late in the evening after the Irish Tradition reunion extravaganza that I sold the only two batches of cookies I ever have – to Wendy Newton, who wanted them to give to a hospitalized friend. I gladly baked the cookies and sent them off to her friend with her and my best wishes. But there was one thing I made sure of before I turned my oven on. I got paid in full, in advance.

## The Dublin Man

I'm really not sure what I was expecting when I walked into the Ice House that Monday morning in July 1986, or for that matter exactly why I was there. It wasn't my first time at the Augusta Irish Week, or even my first time in the Ice House, a hundred-year-old stone silo sunk in the side of one of West Virginia's typically steep hills. I had learned the year before – when I first came to this Irish music version of the summer band camps I'd gone to in high school – that the Ice House was party central for the week, the scene of all the late night drinking and music. (Unlike high school band camp, the drinking at Augusta didn't have to be done undercover. I'm not sure if that made the beer taste better or worse, not having the feel of getting away with something every time you took a chug.) It also wasn't the first time I'd seen Frank Harte. The year before, when I was there taking Robbie O'Connell's guitar class, Frank was there as well, teaching ballads. But he lost his voice very early in the week, which has to be a singer's worst nightmare – and even worse for a singer who's supposed to be teaching others how to sing. Yet I remember walking past the Halliehurst porch one afternoon that week and seeing that Frank had brought his class outside to enjoy the nice weather. He was teaching them the songs by whistling the air to them as they read the words off a page in front of them. I think it was then that I decided to take his class if I came back the next year.

A year later, I had good reason to be questioning that decision. Although I was trying to be a singer, until then I had never sung without someone or something around me to shield me (and more importantly, my listeners) from my solo voice. Whether it was other voices in the choir or my own attempts at guitar accompaniment, there had always been something there for me to take shelter behind, so as not to be so…out there all alone. But Frank Harte was a man who not only sang unaccompanied, he disparaged accompanists. And when I gazed around the circle of seven or eight of us who had gathered around Frank in the dark recesses of the Ice House that morning, I saw mainly singers – most of them women – who were serious about the songs. Not poseurs like me. I was clearly out of my league. And this week was supposed to be my *vacation*?

At this point, all I knew of Irish music was the songs. The dancing and then the tunes were still yet to come. And after a few hours with Frank I realized that although I thought I knew a little about Irish songs, I really didn't know much at all. Frank handed us all a half-inch-thick bound stack of pages, each of which contained the typed-out words to a song. He would flip through his copy until a song caught his eye, and then he'd begin to sing it. Usually but not always, before he'd start he'd say *Are you switched on?* so that we could get our cassette decks running. And almost as many times as he'd start a song, he'd stop after a line or two to change to a lower key. As he often said, *You never know until you reach the highest note in a song whether you're in the right key…and by then it's too late.* In between the songs, there'd be ad hoc lectures on any and all aspects of Irish culture and history, inspired by whatever song had just finished or was about to come next. Sometimes instead of singing it himself Frank would play a recording of his source for a song, none of which were the familiar Clancy Brothers or Tommy Makem but instead names like Margaret Barry or Robert Cinnamond or Geordie Hanna or Eddie Butcher that I'd never heard before. Fascinating stuff, and after a while I just left my recorder switched on for everything and not just Frank's singing.

Then on the second day the class dynamic changed. Not that he was out of songs and stories himself – indeed, he'd barely scratched the surface, as I'd learn in years to come – but it was time for those who had gathered around him to sing. And it wasn't a voluntary option, either. One by one each of us would be put on the spot, until Frank tired of us and moved on to the next victim. I had two things that saved me in this process: I was not a woman, and although I could sing I was not really a singer, which became clear soon enough. I really don't recall if I even actually had to sing during this inquisition process or if those two facts were just so patently obvious that Frank just passed me by. Either way, I found myself able to sit back and watch the process unfold without much personal pain.

Frank had two approaches he'd take as he put each singer through the wringer. Sometimes he'd have them sing one of their songs, perhaps the "party piece" that any singer (or as I'd come to learn, *anyone* who dares to come to a gathering of musicians, dancers or folks with an Irish bent) needs to have in their back pocket at all times. That, or perhaps a song that they'd do on stage if they did gigs. Other times, he'd pick a song from his book and have the singer do a verse or two from it, offer his critique, and then lather, rinse, repeat. This was how Mary Lee, who had been singing quite successfully for a good long while with her band up in Providence, Rhode Island, ended up singing for Frank several verses from a ballad called *Andrew Rose* that was all about the cruel treatment endured over a hundred years ago by a poor young Irish man who had been pressed into service in the British navy.

*Andrew Rose he was a sailor,*
*His sufferings now I will explain.*

*It was on a voyage from the Barbados,*
*On board a vessel called Martha Jane.*

*CHORUS*
*Oh, think about his cruel treatment,*
*Without a friend to interpose.*
*How they whipped and mangled, gagged and strangled*
*That British sailor Andrew Rose.*

*The captain trained his dogs to bite him,*
*While Rose for mercy he did pray.*
*And on the deck, his flesh in mouthfuls,*
*Torn by the dogs it lay.*

*The captain ordered him to swallow*
*A thing thereof I shall not name.*
*The sailors all grew sick with horror*
*On board the vessel Martha Jane.*

On and on the song went, for 15 verses in all. And after Mary Lee had sung each one, there would be no praise, no compliment, no kind word from Frank. Instead, she'd be told that her voice – the same voice that had delighted untold numbers of listeners and made her band local heroes in their hometown – was "queer" (or as Frank said it, "quare.") Not that it was off pitch, or badly phrased, or anything else that could be easily fixed. Just *You have a quare voice. Now, sing it again.* There was a happy ending for the British sailor Andrew Rose that day, although not until the fifteenth verse when the captain finally got his due. But not so for Mary Lee. By the time we broke for lunch, she was on the verge of tears. Her happy ending, or at least some small measure of redemption, didn't occur until after lunch. That was when the daily "lunchtime concert", a fixture at Augusta, took place. The entire assembly of Irish Week – including a large contingent of Elderhostel folks, who Mick Moloney always called "Hostile Elders" because of their propensity to question each and every little thing said by himself or any of the others lined up to give lectures to them all day long – would gather in the largest classroom on campus to hear a few songs and tunes from the Irish Week staff. A great way to burn off an hour before the afternoon class session started, at least from the students' perspective. But many of the teachers had better ideas on how to spend that time, so it was frequently a struggle for Mick to find enough of them around to fill all the time. And so it happened that Mary Lee's band got called up to do a song, one she had written herself about the plight of mill workers in her Rhode Island home town. To great acclaim from the assembly, this performance mostly – but not quite – absolved her of her sins that same morning. At the least it cheered her up a bit and got her back in the Ice House that afternoon.

As that day reached its end, two things stuck with me. First was a profound sense of gratitude that *I* had not been the one called on to sing. But even more compelling was the juxtaposition of the singer and the song that I had witnessed that morning, and before I went to bed that night these words had emerged to fit the air to the song Andrew Rose that had been pounded into my brain that day.

*Come all you singers, pay attention*
*And listen for a while to me*
*While I tell you all a dreadful story*
*That happened during Irish Week.*

*Now, Mary Lee she was a singer*
*From way up north in Rhode Eye-Land.*
*She came to the hills of West Virginia*
*To study with the Dublin man.*

CHORUS
*Oh, think about her cruel treatment.*
*Without a friend to intercede,*
*How he nagged and hassled, mocked and frazzled*
*That sweet young singer Mary Lee.*

*Now on that day down in the Ice House,*
*Amidst the stench of week old beer,*
*She sat down at the foot of the great man*
*Thinking from him wond'rous songs she'd hear.*

*She waited with anticipation,*
*Her tape recorder running strong,*
*When he turned around so as to face her*
*And said "Mary Lee, sing us a song."*

CHORUS
*Oh, think about her cruel treatment.*
*Without a friend to intercede,*
*How he nagged and hassled, mocked and frazzled*
*That sweet young singer Mary Lee.*

Said Mary Lee, "I don't yet know one,
But I will sing one when I can."
But if she thought that might dissuade him
She did not know the Dublin man.

For he continued to berate her,
Until at last she sang a verse.
Said he, "For sure you have a quare voice,
Although I think I have heard worse.

CHORUS
Oh, think about her cruel treatment.
Without a friend to intercede,
How he nagged and hassled, mocked and frazzled
That sweet young singer Mary Lee.

He then forced her to sing another,
A song thereof I shall not name.
He forced her to shout out the chorus.
That Dublin man, he has no shame.

Said he, "If you want to sing ballads
You must do something with your voice.
Or else you'll have to twang on guitars,
And that would be an awful choice."

*CHORUS*
*Oh, think about her cruel treatment.*
*Without a friend to intercede,*
*How he nagged and hassled, mocked and frazzled*
*That sweet young singer Mary Lee.*

*Then – good for her – there came the lunch break,*
*And afterwards the daily show*
*Where mainly just to hear the Great Man*
*All the Elderhostel people go.*

*There Mary Lee brought a surprise,*
*A song that came from her own pen.*
*The crowd went wild! She sure stole the show*
*From Rob, Mick and the Dublin man.*

*CHORUS*
*Oh, think about her cruel treatment.*
*Without a friend to intercede,*
*How he nagged and hassled, mocked and frazzled*
*That sweet young singer Mary Lee.*

*So singers, hear and heed this lesson.*
*Like Mary Lee, get in and fight.*
*But don't tune out the thoughts of this man,*
*For you never know…he might be right.*

As the week progressed, these few words I had put together spread throughout the other students in the class, almost but not quite like wildfire (since Al Gore had not yet invented the Internet and we didn't even have access to a Xerox we could use for free.) Seemingly without correlation, there were no more incidents of outright torture in Frank's class. But whoever it was that said *what goes around, comes around* was right, as I was to find out on Friday morning, which was the last real class session of the week. Frank was going around the circle allowing everyone to sing a song if they wanted to, and someone said *John has a song*. Frank's eyes lit up, and he said *Ah yes, I have heard of this song*. Before I had a chance to deny anything, I was forced to sing. Considering what had happened to the subject of my song just a few days before, I thought for sure that my fate was sealed. I shuddered to think of the reaction that would come from the Dublin man when I was done singing, but to my great surprise and relief he laughed. My relief was short-lived though, because once his peal of laughter was over, the next words out of his mouth were *You will sing this after lunch*.

And so it was that I became the final act of that week's series of lunchtime concerts, in front of all my peers, the Irish Week teachers, and the Hostile Elders, singing what Frank introduced as "a scurrilous song" written by one of his loyal pupils. Somewhere there exist tape recordings of me singing this song, which I hope never see the light of day. I know that somewhere in my house sits a box with one such cassette, that I know I will not be releasing if I should ever happen to run across it. But I'm sure I wasn't the only one who was switched on as I sang, so I can only hope for mercy from any others that may be lurking out there. The words are the relevant part of any sin I may have committed that day, and by writing them down here I have now done penance twice for them. But none of the principals would consider this drama sinful, I know that for a fact. Mary Lee survived and thrived, better for the experience. One year later, I ran into her at the Willie Clancy Week in Miltown Malbay, and we raised a glass to Frank. She even returned to the scene of the crime in Elkins some years later to take Frank's class again. As for Frank, the notoriety gained from this incident only served to cement his reputation as The Great One, a moniker by which he was known and loved at Augusta for much of the next two decades. As for me, by daring to write this scurrilous song about him I was raised from the anonymity I had when I came into Frank's class. I was not a singer; that was clear to all. But I had made a friend, someone I would see again almost every year until he died in 2005.

I kept coming back to Augusta every summer for something like fifteen years. (The phrase "get a life" may have been coined with me in mind.) I think I took Frank's class one more time, with much less drama than the first time around (sequels, as we all know, never being as good as the original) and then I moved on to other pursuits where I had more talent to put in play, first set dancing and then flute playing. But each year when I arrived in Elkins, Frank was there as a fixture – except for the one year he missed when he was having heart bypass surgery in Ireland. (Typical of Frank, after the surgery he was unchanged – including his diet. I gave him a lift into downtown Elkins for lunch once after his surgery, so we could escape the horrors of the campus dining hall. His order? Burger, fries, shake.) Frank's presence clearly gave context to the week, more so perhaps than anyone else other than Mick Moloney, who founded the week in the first place. And the constant one-upmanship between Mick and Frank, rooted as it was in their mutual respect for each other, kept the classes, concerts and other activities light and fun, while in no way diminishing the serious business of imparting the tradition to a bunch of Yanks, which indeed was the point of it all. From Frank we learned both the nuances of Irish history and the impact of current events in Ireland, both of which are not easily accessible to those of us who live across the pond but want to think of ourselves as "of Ireland." The medium of transmission was the songs, of which Frank had thousands, and the words of introduction to the song, of which Frank often had many more than there were words in the song he was getting ready to sing. As many words as there were, not one of them was superfluous or wasted.

Frank's point of view was never hidden, subtle or nuanced. As he often said, in a phrase that's become his epitaph, *Those in power write the history, those who suffer write the songs. And given our history, we have an awful lot of songs.* He was every inch a Republican (that would be an Irish Republican, which is a vastly different animal than an American Republican) but in no way political. He wanted basic justice and freedom for everyone, the compromises of politics be damned. His desires for freedom didn't just apply to people, they applied to songs as well. He frequently quoted the poet Brendan Kennelly, who wrote *All songs are living ghosts and long for a living voice.* Frank would sing any song, as long as it was a good song. It didn't have to be Irish, or even fit precisely with his own worldview. He sang Orange songs with gusto. If someone popped a head into his class or one of his lectures, he would invariably ask if they had a song. Whatever they might sing in response to that query, he would listen. And if it was good, he would take it and make it his own.

For Frank, songs were the underpinning of life, and the basis of all music. It all came back to the song. Frank's influence on and generosity with singers like Karan Casey is well known, but he was equally as generous with instrumental musicians. The young fiddlers Jesse Smith and Jim Eagan, among others, went to Frank for slow airs prior to competing in the fleadhs in New York and in Ireland. I remember Jesse taking a strong third in slow airs at the Fleadh Cheoil in Clonmel in 1994. I was there and watched the competition, and in my opinion he should have won. For the slow airs championship, a competitor needs to have eight airs prepared, although only three of them will actually get played. Jesse got his airs from Frank and from the great Derry fiddler Eugene O'Donnell, probably the two best sources available.

For about ten years I had the chance to spend huge blocks of time with Frank as I gave him rides back and forth to Elkins from his daughter's house outside of Washington DC. It was a drive that normally took about four hours each way – except for the first time. We loaded up the car outside the Gribble Dorm after breakfast on Saturday morning (or maybe it was already afternoon, mornings in general being anathema to musicians, especially on Saturdays after Irish Week.) Before we left town I needed to gas up, and this being long before pay-at-the-pump was introduced to West Virginia, that necessitated a stroll inside the general store that was attached to the gas station. While waiting for me to pay, Frank caught a glimpse of some fishing lures ("baits" as he called them) on display and bought a few. But this also brought the general idea of shopping into his head, and in my weakened state after a week of little sleep I found myself agreeing to a stop at the local WalMart on our way out of town. This was early in that chain's existence, so I don't think there was anyone to greet us yet as we walked in the door. But that didn't stop Frank from deciding to stay a spell after we got inside. I think it was at least two hours before he was done with his shopping spree. His cart was filled with a motley collection of stuff, a lot of it for others than himself. Blue jeans for his sons back in Ireland. A fishing pole to go with the baits. Apparently *everything* was cheaper at WalMart than in Ireland, and he was clearly giving no thought to how he'd get the stuff on the plane back to Dublin, much less how it would all go into the trunk of my car with all of the luggage we already had there.

But most of that two hours in WalMart was spent contemplating a single purchase that he ultimately didn't make – a pair of Dr. Scholl's sandals. Uglier than Birkenstocks at a fraction of the price, except they didn't have Frank's size in stock that day. I finally managed to get him out of the store and on the road by mentioning that I thought there was a K-Mart in Harrisonburg where we'd be stopping for lunch. Maybe they'd have the shoes there. I was secretly hoping that in the two hours it would take to drive to Harrisonburg he'd forget about the shoes, but no such luck. It turned out that they did have the ugly Dr. Scholl's sandals at K-Mart, and they even had them in Frank's size. But they cost a whole dollar more than they did at WalMart! Just then, Frank remembered seeing a WalMart somewhere near the place we'd had lunch. *We must go there,* he said. With nothing to lose but another half hour on the road, I had no room for argument and off to WalMart we went. Fortunately, the shoes were there, in stock and in size and at the advertised low price. Frank didn't bother to get them bagged, he wore them out. Our next stop was his daughter Sinead's house in Chevy Chase, and when we arrived at her doorstep some nine hours after we'd left Elkins and at least five hours after we were due there, she took one look down at his feet and said with disgust *Oh, Frank!*

With Frank in the car there was no need to keep the radio on or a CD in the player, since any time we weren't talking he'd be lilting the words of whatever song was on his mind at the time. A perennial topic of conversation between us was the shared sad lot in life we had as single men – although, technically, Frank wasn't actually single. Divorce being illegal then in Ireland, he had split up with his wife but was still living in a small house on the same property, right next to where she lived in the house he had built for them to raise their family. It was a civilized "divorce" – indeed he told me he went over to her house every morning for his tea. I never told him this, but I would be quite happy to have that kind of bachelorhood instead of what I have now, where I have to make my own tea! In our chats as we wound our way through the hills of West Virginia Frank always managed to put me – a resident of the US capital, the most political city in the world – to shame with his observations and insights about the inner workings of the US government and its impact on the rest of the world. He was quick to call out hypocrites, ideologues and those who would take advantage of others, but he always managed to do it in a gentle and usually humorous way. The drive back and forth from Washington to Elkins was usually the best part of Irish Week for me, so much so that even after I quit going there for the whole week I would drive out at the end just for the chance to give Frank a lift back. Over time, I even figured out how to keep the drive to the four hours it was supposed to be. If Frank would notice the old barns by the side of the road and say *Sometime we must stop so I can photograph these barns,* I would agree and say *Next time*. Somehow, by the next time it would be forgotten.

Even though I did make about eight trips to Ireland while I knew Frank, I almost always saw him when he was in the States. When I was in Ireland I'd typically be in the West, where the music's the strongest, and the few times I did make it to Dublin he was away. But in 2001 I saw him at the Willie Clancy Week, where he was on the program giving a lecture on song. This was nice and much deserved, but it also signaled that his health was beginning to fail, since the main reason he typically wasn't at Willie Week was that he would already be in America doing his summer tour of music camps and visiting his daughter and her family. By 2003 when I was next in Ireland he had made his farewell to the Augusta Irish Week and it didn't look like he'd be coming again across the pond. So I made a point on that trip of going to Dublin, and Frank was gracious enough to take me into his house for a couple of days. My friend Tina Eck had stayed with Frank on a visit a year or so before that and ended up taking him to the hospital while she was there, so I was a little uncertain as to what manner of adventure might await me when I arrived.

I started my trip that August at the Feakle Festival in east Clare. I gave Frank a call from there to confirm my arrival time in Dublin and get the directions. *Park on the street outside my front gate,* he said, *and leave nothing in the car or it will be stolen in an instant.* After three hours on the road and little trouble thanks to my detailed street map of Dublin, I arrived in the little village called Chapelizod and started looking for his house, number 94 Martin's Row. I drove up the street, checking off the numbers one by one, but when I reached what should have been his neighborhood I found nothing but a long concrete wall, covered with vegetation, hard up against the sidewalk and punctuated by the odd gate here and there. Taking Frank's instruction to mind, I parked the car as close to gate #94 as I could get and yanked my huge suitcase and the smaller bag containing the flute and concertina from the boot. The car I'd rented was so small that I'd had to put the back seat down in order to get my bags in there at all, so everything would have been on full display if I'd left it in there. *When, oh when will I ever learn to pack lightly?* I thought as I struggled down the street to the gate.

I could see over the top of the gate that there was a house about ten yards behind, but no bell to ring. I knocked, but all that did was set a dog to barking. After a few minutes of this, I decided I had no other choice but to go inside and knock on the front door of the house. I popped open the gate and was immediately set upon by the dog for the full sniff. Never having been a dog person myself – I was deathly afraid of them throughout my childhood and still felt on edge any time there was one nearby – this was not a pleasant experience at all. I looked up and saw a woman who was gardening near the front door of the house giving me and my massive luggage a strange look. *I'm looking for Frank Harte,* I said. She pointed down toward a small house past the garden she was tending, maybe thirty yards from where I stood. I immediately figured out what I'd done. This was the house Frank had built, where his estranged wife lived, and it was her that I'd encountered. Frank was next door. So I trudged downhill along the grassy patch next to the garden, lugging my giant bags with me, dog barking and sniffing closely after me the whole way. By the time I reached the house, the dog's barking had attracted Frank's attention and he looked down from the upstairs window to see what was going on. *John! What are you doing, and how did you get there?*

It turned out that except for the lack of a number on his house, I could have rung Frank's front doorbell right from the sidewalk, and not had to deal with the dog at all – the dog that, once I asked, turned out to be a Rottweiler. Good thing I didn't ask until I was safely inside the house! From the street, Frank's house looked like any other small one-story stone cottage on the end of an attached row of them, just like you see all over Ireland. A brick-framed door sat in between two brick-framed windows, and the whole house was maybe 25 feet wide, if that. Inside the front door was a small foyer, with the door to the bedroom straight ahead and a spiral staircase to the left. Walking down the stairs took you into the part of the house you couldn't see from the street, as it was built into the side of a hill. At the bottom of the stairs was the room that Frank used as an office, that was taken up mostly by a large drawing-board of a desk – Frank having been an architect and university lecturer in his day job. Now he was retired from that, and instead of drawings an old Apple computer sat on the desk, containing a database that linked together the words, sources, supporting photos, articles and such for the thousands of songs he had collected in his life. Shelves on the wall held recordings of many of the songs, all indexed from his database. It was here that Frank wrote the voluminous sleeve notes – miniature history books, to tell the truth – for the CDs he'd been producing with a frenzy ever since he retired from the day job. He'd released two of them before I was there, *1798 The First Year of Liberty* and the two-CD set *My Name is Napoleon Bonaparte,* and had just finished work on the third one, called *The Hungry Voice: The Song Legacy of Ireland's Great Hunger.*

In the back of the house – which on this level was really the front – was the living/dining room that held the sofa where I'd be bunking, and beyond that an airy but small kitchen. This opened onto the back garden where I'd made my entrance, which sat right on the banks of the River Liffey – really not much more than a wide stream there, with a heavily-wooded promontory across from Frank's house that turned the whole property into what seemed like a nature preserve stuck right in the midst of an increasingly urbanized little village nestled hard up against Dublin's giant Phoenix Park. The Celtic Tiger was still roaring at the time, and beyond the trees could be seen the tops of cranes being used to build condos that Frank told me were selling for one million euro. (I feel sorry for anyone who might have bought one of them. That is, unless it was an Irish government or banking official, in which case I feel schadenfreude. You could probably buy a million of those condos for one euro now.)

Frank was a serious man who did not take himself seriously, not in the least. The Great One – his moniker in Elkins – was the perfect description of Frank, because it worked in the ironic sense but was also true in the literal sense. The inside of his house was crammed full of books – some shelved, some just stacked, on all manner of topics. Works of art were on display on walls and floors inside the house, and a large piece of sculpture sat outside in the back garden. Scattered about on shelves along with the books, recordings and knick-knacks were photos of Frank with notable folks like Pete Seeger. There was an architectural sensibility to the place – no surprise given that Frank was an architect himself. Some might have quibbled over his housekeeping – Tina in fact told me that one thing she did on her own visit there, in addition to taking Frank to the hospital, was to give the place a thorough sweep-up – but it definitely met my own bachelor standard of cleanliness. I certainly felt no urge to tidy up while I was there, but instead spent the three days I was in Dublin seeing the sights by day (with assistance from a back-of-the-envelope map Frank drew up for me) and going to sessions by night.

Frank accompanied me to the first session I went to, on a Monday night at The Cobblestone, one of Dublin's legendary session venues that featured a different cast of players every night of the week. Frank went there often, even though it was several miles away from his house. In fact, at that stage of his life it was pretty much his "local." I sat down with the young players who were circled around the table in the front window. (I say "young" because they were in their twenties while I was then almost fifty, but they were all probably much older in the music than I was – or at least I'd like to think, because they were all better players than me.) Frank took a stool at the bar, directly behind the session circle. As the night went on, he chatted with any number of other punters who were also spending the evening in the establishment. They all knew who he was, but it became clear that none of the young session players did – for if they had known there was a singer in their midst, especially one as august as Frank, proper session protocol would have had them call for a song at some point during the proceedings. Yet no one did, which bothered Frank not at all. Clearly he had sung in that pub on some occasions before, and he surely would again. But a night at the local was every bit as good without a song.

I'm not sure when or how much Frank slept during the three days I was there, because he was up most of the night puttering around in his bedroom directly above the couch I was sleeping on, worn out from traipsing around Dublin all day and playing tunes at night. Fortunately the constant sound of the Liffey flowing by just outside provided some white noise to help me nod off. Perhaps he napped some during the day while I was out, but for the most part he was up and active, running errands and working out the logistics for some future recording projects and gigs. He didn't seem slowed much at all by age (he was then around 70), yet when it came time for me to leave Dublin and head back to Clare to finish out my vacation, I had the strong sense that I might not see him again. I knew he would not likely make it back to America, and I was unsure about when I'd be back in Ireland – although I had no idea it would be the current nine years and counting. So it was with sadness rather than surprise that I heard less than two years later that Frank's daughter Orla had come by the house one afternoon to find him slumped over the big desk at the foot of the spiral stairs, dead of a heart attack. He'd been on the phone less than 30 minutes before, working out some final details on his recording *There's Gangs of Them Digging*, which was released after his death in his memory.

Even though Frank is no longer with us, I still feel his presence in my life all the time – and I know I'm not alone in that. He left a great recorded legacy that gets played frequently, and anytime someone on Facebook links to a YouTube video of Frank, the comments flow freely. I'm certainly more of a tune person than a song person myself, but I hear a lot of songs when I'm out at sessions, concerts and festivals, or listening to Irish trad shows on streaming audio on my iPhone. And it's rare that I hear a new song from some singer's repertoire and don't end up thinking that I first heard it sung by Frank at some time over the years. That's especially true if it happens to be a really good song. And as much as I've always been struck by the power of the words in the songs Frank sang, as a musician myself I'm even more inspired by the musicianship of his singing. His phrasing, his pitch (once he settled on a key, of course), his ability to use the notes as well as the words to convey the emotion within the song, all were impeccable. I find myself striving to emulate all that as I play tunes on the flute, but I know I fall short. Still, I think my playing is better for the effort. The fact that I can still gain inspiration from Frank's memory in my flute playing along with, really, everything else

I do in life truly says how privileged I was to have him as a friend. I recall hearing that at his funeral he was laid out in a simple pine box that had inscribed on it the words "Frank Harte, National Treasure." In this same box he was cremated after the funeral. This was typical of the man, creating a monument to the great contributions he had made during his life but doing it in an insignificant and impermanent way. Sic transit gloria mundi.

As Frank often said, in the words of Brendan Kennelly, *All songs are living ghosts and long for a living voice.* Although Frank may be gone, as long as his memory lives and the songs are sung, his voice is still alive. And I know it will be alive for a long, long time. But I'm sad that I'll never have the chance to stop along a road in West Virginia so he can photograph those barns. I wish there was going to be a next time.

*Frank Harte singing at the grave of the piper Willie Clancy. Milltown Malbay, Co. Clare, July 2001.*

# The Party

Public events like sessions and ceilis can often be great for the music and the craic, but no matter how great they are they never will rise to the level of a really good house party. Fortunately for me, ever since I first got into Irish music and dance I've had friends who throw great parties. It's really an art. I tried throwing a semi-annual tune party myself for a few years after I moved from my small condo to a house that is big enough to hold a crowd, and although there were some good times now and then, things just never seemed to really click. Either I would pick a night that too many people had gigs or invitations to better parties, or the weather was bad, or people got lost trying to find my house in the days before MapQuest and GPS. It was always something. Maybe I just don't have the magic touch, like my friend Tina who always throws a great party filled with musicians, artists, actors, poets and friends from all different corners of the world. Thanks be to God that she doesn't ever lose track of my e-mail address when it's time to send the invitations out!

But as good as Tina's parties are, or even Jesse Winch's parties, or lately Patrick and Crystal's parties, none can compare with the parties Mike and Marleen Denney used to throw when they lived in an old rowhouse on the fringes of Capitol Hill. There is one particular species of party that's better than all the rest – the after-party. Mike and Marleen were champions of the after-party. All it took was a concert of some stature happening somewhere around town – like Mick Moloney's annual Gaston Hall concert, another event that like the Glen Echo/Wolf Trap Festival is sadly no more – and the word would go out: party afterward at Mike and Marleen's. Why, one time they even appropriated Donna Long's house up in Baltimore for a party after a boatload of Cape Breton musicians landed in the harbor there for a few days. Any party thrown by Mike and Marleen was always guaranteed to be legendary. But there was one in particular that will never, ever be surpassed.

The year was 1994, the heady days of the first Clinton administration. I was heavily involved in the production of the Irish Festival, which had only a year or so before that made its big move from the run-down Glen Echo site to the spiffy grounds of Wolf Trap. Mike Denney was the festival director and a major player on the Irish scene in these parts. He was also almost single-handedly responsible for Cape Breton music having made its way to the DC area. In the process of pushing the festival to ever bigger and better artistic standards, Michael had hooked us up with Nick Spitzer, a folklorist and radio guy who was then affiliated with the Smithsonian. It was a tight little web of connections that ensured a steady stream of great musicians coming through the area throughout the year, but particularly during the St. Patrick's Day season. This particular year, the convergence of Clinton, Denney and Spitzer resulted in a never-to-be-equaled St. Patrick's Day experience for me and perhaps a hundred or so other folks. Here's how it all played out.

As they still do today, the National Geographic would put on a sporadic series of concerts in their Grosvenor Auditorium downtown, and St. Patrick's Day was generally the occasion for an Irish concert. That year, they had Altan for two shows – one geared for the just-after-work crowd, and one later in the evening. I chose to attend the early show myself, because of what Nick Spitzer had going on at Wolf Trap later that night. Nick was at the time in the midst of a three or four year long series of concerts/radio programs called Folk Masters, which he produced at The Barns of Wolf Trap for later broadcast on NPR stations. Each year, he put on 13 or so concerts at The Barns, covering the full spectrum of ethnic folk music across America. I went to a lot of these shows (and indeed one year I saw them all, since I volunteered to be the product sales guy in the lobby for the full series) and heard a lot of incredible music, but obviously the ones I liked the best were the one or two shows a year where he featured Irish music. In 1994 for St. Patrick's Day he had put together a spectacular Irish-Cape Breton-Appalachian crossover show, featuring Mick Moloney, Eileen Ivers, Seamus Egan and Eugene O'Donnell doing their Green Fields of America thing, Buddy MacMaster and Dave MacIsaac from Cape Breton, and Tennessee long-bow fiddler Ralph Blizard and his New Southern Ramblers. (Of course, all of these artists had already appeared at the Irish Festival over the years, thanks to the tight web of connection between Mike Denney, Nick Spitzer and Mick Moloney.) Mike and Marleen had put out the word that there would be a party at their house this St. Patrick's night, so after going to the Geographic to hear Altan and then out to Wolf Trap for Nick Spitzer's show, with a batch of big cookies in hand, around midnight I made my way down the mean streets of near-Anacostia to their house.

Nowadays, whenever I go to a house party I usually spend most or all of the evening playing tunes, but back then I was so new to the flute that I don't think I even had it with me. At Mike and Marleen's parties it was always a treat to be able to stand right behind the circle of real musicians playing together informally, just to see how it was supposed to be done. And of course, this also included the essential lesson that sessions aren't just about the tunes, but also (and maybe even more so) about the personal interactions between the players. So on this particular night, I was entertained by the sight of Eileen Ivers and Ralph Blizard trading barnyard sounds on the fiddle for about a half hour. Then things began to heat up in the dining room, where Mike and Marleen had installed a piano that they bought just for parties, since neither of them played. Buddy MacMaster took out his fiddle and started in on some long sets of sweet Cape Breton tunes. It was about this time that the whole party got kicked up a notch, thanks to Bill Clinton. Unlike either of the Bush administrations, which thought Ireland was only good as a refueling spot for troops headed to Eye-rack or Afghanistan, the Clintons did so much for Ireland that they were treated like Gods there whenever they'd visit the Emerald Isle. So every year on St. Patrick's Day during the Clinton years, the White House was the site of a big hooley, with the Irish ambassador and hosts of other Irish and Irish-American luminaries on hand. There was always music involved, and this particular year among others the musicians included Altan, Sharon Shannon and our local hero Billy McComiskey. Somehow the word got spread around at the White House that there was a party happening later that night, and what do you know but a few of the folks from the White House hooley ended up wandering over to Mike and Marleen's. Not the President or Hillary or the ambassador, mind you. But there were a couple of them that you may have heard of. For instance:

While we were gathered around the dining room listening to Buddy MacMaster play, word started filtering back from the front of the house that Richard Harris had just walked in. I thought to myself *Self, maybe you should wander up front and check this out*. But I quickly came to my senses when I remembered *Hey, Buddy MacMaster is playing right here in front of me*! I figured that if he really was in the house, Richard Harris would come back my way soon enough, and indeed he eventually did. Now, as it happens I had just seen Richard Harris the night before on Letterman, where he was wearing a brightly-patterned jacket and told the tale of having it made as a memento from the blanket that he and some woman had made love on. He was not so distinctly dressed this night, and I can't claim to have had a conversation with him in the midst of the crowd. But I was standing within a few feet of him for a while, if that counts for anything. At one point late in the evening he got into a drunken conversation with Eugene O'Donnell that resulted in him saying to Eugene *If you'll play the Derry Air, I'll sing Carrickfergus!* So Eugene picked up his fiddle and started the air, and as he played on the crowded, noisy house fell so silent that you could have heard a pin drop. It was as beautiful as anything I had ever heard Eugene play. Then, when Eugene was done Richard Harris launched into the song about how he wished he was in Carrickfergus. And by God, he made me wish he was in Carrickfergus too, because his singing was God-awful. But I shouldn't have been surprised at that, because after all my youth had been scarred by hearing a recording of his called MacArthur Park.

There was also this beautiful young Irish woman there that night, black-haired and in an off-the-shoulder little black dress that really accentuated her charms, if you get my drift. When someone told me who she was, I realized that I'd heard of her but didn't know much about her other than her name. Roma Downey. Several years later, the whole world would hear of her, after she got touched by an angel. (Lucky her. Irish boys of her generation got touched by the priest.) I can't claim to have had any conversation with her, either, because I was younger then and found talking and drooling at the same time difficult. (I probably should start figuring that out, though, before I get too much older and find myself drooling even when there aren't any beautiful women nearby.) But I do recall standing a respectable distance away from her when she was introduced to Eugene O'Donnell, and hearing her loudly and drunkenly exclaim *You're from Derry? I'm from Derry too!* before throwing herself all over him. I wish *I* was from Derry...

The director Jim Sheridan, who had recently made his name with the film My Left Foot, was there that night as well. I knew who he was, but I didn't talk with him either. And being a director rather than an actor, he didn't have any theatrical moments for me to recall like the lovely Ms. Downey and the unfortunately-voiced Mr. Harris. But I'm sure if I had chatted with him at all, I'd have found him quite witty and urbane, as all Irish men are from birth. Unless they're drunk, of course, when they tend to become rather uncouth, but still quite witty (and sometimes more so).

And lest you think that all I did that night was listen to great tunes and not talk with famous Irish people, around five in the morning I did lay down on the couch in Mike and Marleen's front room for a little nap. Waking up groggily a few minutes later, from the corner of my eye I saw Sharon Shannon and Seamus Egan bouncing around like they were in a mosh pit. I think they were playing hacky-sack or something. Was I dreaming? Or just drunk? I don't remember. But it was a memorable night nonetheless.

## On the Holy Ground Once More

I was not born on The Holy Ground, and neither were any recent-enough ancestors of mine that would qualify me to apply for Irish citizenship. Yet somehow whenever I step off the plane in Shannon or Dublin Airport I feel like I am home. The first time I ever had that feeling was on the morning of the Fourth of July 1987. After an all-night flight from Boston, I stepped off the Northwest Airlines plane at around seven in the morning into what would turn out to be a glorious Irish summer day. In those convenient years before global warming was proclaimed as a truth, that meant there was not a cloud in the sky, the temperature peaked at around 18 degrees – that's Celsius, y'all; in Fahrenheit it was around 65 – and there was a stiff 20 knot wind. (Contrast this with my most recent visit in August 2003, when temps were in the 90s – Fahrenheit, thankfully – in a country where air conditioning is virtually unheard of.) After stopping in the Shannon Airport cafeteria for my first real Irish breakfast fry, I picked up my bags and rental car and headed out for almost two weeks of the adventure that is driving (not to mention shifting gears) on the left.

The first episode of which occurred that very afternoon, when I took a notion to visit the Cliffs of Moher. I started off by following a map, but quickly eschewed that approach when I caught a glimpse of the Cliffs way off in front of me and decided I could just as easily get there by relying on my own internal GPS – although the GPS not having been invented yet, I had no idea then that that was what I was doing. Actually, that decision led to my undoing. With the Cliffs always in sight in front of me, I turned from narrow West Clare road onto narrower West Clare road, until at last the road I was on was barely one car-width wide. Driving up this road, after a while I saw a house in front of me and came to the realization that I was driving up someone's driveway. But as it happened, there was a car right behind me. I thought that this must surely be the homeowner whose property I was on, and if he didn't shoot me for trespassing when we reached the end of the driveway, I could do the un-manly thing and ask him for directions to the Cliffs. (Of course, this being my first visit to Ireland, I had no realization yet that the answer would have been something like *Ahh, the Cliffs. You wouldn't want to be going there from here now, you see. But if you did...*until ten minutes later I would have totally forgotten where it was I was wanting to go in the first place, with the directions still going on of course.) But this little drama never had the chance to play out, since when we both reached the end of the drive, the car behind me stopped, turned around (which took a good bit of maneuvering, given the narrow road) and headed out. He was as lost as I was! I had no choice but to turn around and head back out myself. The other car being long gone by the time it took me to execute my U-turn, I was heading back alone down the narrow driveway, driving straight down the middle of the road. As eventually the road began to widen, I did the natural thing and slid on over to the right side of the road. Having the road – and, it seemed, the entire county – to myself, I was looking right and left at the scenery until I happened to glance back at the road – only to see a giant farm tractor barreling right at me. Okay, "barreling" is a bit of an exaggeration, since I can actually crawl faster than it was moving, but the farmer sitting on top of it did have a bit of a *WTF is that crazy Yank up to?* look on his face, so I slid meekly over to the left side of the road where I belonged, and avoided a nasty collision by mere minutes.

Suitably shamed, I resolved to drive safely for the rest of my time in Ireland, and eventually did find my way to the Cliffs of Moher. Impressive as they are, though – especially on a bright and sunny blue-sky day – the Cliffs were not the reason I came to Ireland. No, I was there to attend the Scoil Samraidh Willie Clancy – a.k.a. the Willie Clancy Summer School, a.k.a. Willie Week – in the nearby village of Miltown Malbay. I remember the first time I ever heard reference to Willie Week. It was a couple of years before this, when I was at Augusta Irish Week for one of the first times, and Robbie O'Connell up on stage mentioned having sung a song at what I thought he was calling the Woolly Clancy Week. I thought it must have been some sort of sheep festival, perhaps involving the Aran sweaters worn by his famous uncles the Clancy Brothers, but I eventually learned that in reality it was something *much* more exciting than that. Or maybe not. So after six months of taking set dancing classes taught by Mike Denney in the Spanish Ballroom at Glen Echo Park, I realized I absolutely had to go to this Willie Week. Unlike probably half the class at Glen Echo, who disappeared after the fifth or sixth straight week of going back and forth, over and over again, from one end of the loooong Spanish Ballroom to the other, as we repeated the distinctive "up on the downbeat" Clare step until we got it right, I had decided I wanted to get it right. Or maybe I just wanted to see what the other three figures of the six-figure Caledonian set were that we didn't have time to get to in Mike Denney's ten-week series of classes. (Unknown to me at the time, there was another benefit from all those weeks of dancing back and forth in the Spanish Ballroom, aside from learning the Clare step. The music for the class was a tape of Billy McComiskey playing the reel The Sally Gardens, starting off slow and then gradually picking up speed. When I picked up the flute several years later, this was the first reel I was able to play, since I already had the tune solidly in my head.) At any rate, I had heard that Willie Week was indeed the one place in the world where I was most likely to get it right, and so there I was.

The whole trip to Ireland had been planned out well in advance, with plane tickets, car hire reservations and B&B booking made at least six months ahead. Never having been to a summer school in Ireland before, I thought that proper planning also would involve pre-registering for the school, so I had mailed off a check for the dollar equivalent of 25 Irish pounds to Harry Hughes in Miltown Malbay to enroll myself in Beginners and Polka Set Dancing class, as was instructed on the little three-fold flyer I had picked up somewhere beforehand (and still have in my photo album). Somehow I had missed the second bit under 'Registration' on the flyer, where it said *nó ar chlarú i Sráid na Cathrach* (or *on registering in Miltown Malbay*). Little did I realize that no one, save for the clueless Yank, actually *pre-*registered for Willie Week. For everyone but the likes of me, it was (and still is today) a pay-at-the-door event, with no one ever turned away. (Of course, pipers being a far different species of folk both then and now, they operate under different rules that do require pre-registering for Willie Week. Part of the mystery of the pipes, I guess.) The fact that I had pre-registered actually slowed down the process of my registration when I went into the lobby of the Community Hall on the Saturday afternoon, since they had to find some record of having received my check. But eventually it was all sorted out and I was issued the little rectangular hand-written name tag (which I also still have) that enabled me to come back to the Community Hall at 10:00 on Monday morning for the set dancing class, where I first met the two teachers, Joe and Siobhan O'Donovan of Cork.

Joe and Siobhan had been asked by the Willie Week founders to start a set dancing class as part of the week about five years before I got there. They taught a beginner class in the Community Hall that first year. Set dancing took off in popularity and additional dancing classes were added, but Joe and Siobhan remained as teachers of the beginner class. This was entirely appropriate, because if ever there was an exception to the rule that "those who can't do, teach" it was Joe and Siobhan. They were both excellent dancers, Joe especially so. And they had the perfect approach to teaching the dances. First, the two of them as a couple would demonstrate and teach the steps to be used in the set, be it the polka and slide step for the sets from Kerry, the reel and jig steps for the sets from Clare, or the hornpipe step that seems to find its way into almost every set. We students would already be formed into sets of four couples on the floor, and with our partners we'd work on the step under the watchful eyes of Joe and Siobhan. Once it looked like everyone was picking up on the step, they'd pull three couples off the floor to come to the front and form a set with the two of them to demonstrate the figure. After running through it a few times while we all watched, the three couples would return to their sets and we'd all run through the figure. Joe would stand up front, on the stage if there was one, and talk us through the figure while Siobhan worked the floor, making sure everyone had it right and gently pushing a couple in the right direction if they got headed off the wrong way. Then, after a bit, would come the words from Joe that would draw everyone to attention. *Are you right, Siobhan? Are you right?* Siobhan would give the nod, the music would start, and we'd be off.

As the class worked its way through first the Kerry Set and then the Caledonian, I must have been doing something right because around Wednesday Siobhan asked me if I would be willing to be part of a set from the beginner's class that they were putting together to lead off the Thursday night concert, which was billed in the little three-fold flyer as "An Evening of Traditional Set Dancing conducted by Joe O'Donovan." This performance turned out to be a series of figures extracted from sets from various areas of Ireland, danced by different sets of dancers most of whom had come in from the countryside specifically for the evening. This was a time when distinctive regional styles of footwork were still a part of set dancing. Comhaltas and the competition ethic have pretty much homogenized things now for the dancing, alas, just as they did with the music, but this evening featured a range of styles from the precision work of a set of elementary school students to the sublime battering of a set of septuagenarians and octogenarians from Labasheeda.

Fortunately the set of dancing tourists doing a figure of the Kerry Set, of which I was a part, danced first in the program and thus was almost (but not quite) obliterated from memory by all of the outstanding and much more traditional dancing that followed. I say "not quite" because there happened to be a crew of documentary film-makers (from Maryland, of all places) wandering around Miltown and filming away all week long. The Thursday night of the dance performance they were camped right up in the front row, stage right. Blessedly my performance ended up on the cutting room floor when they released their 30-minute video about a year later. A real treasure, this video recounts not just the dancing, but all of what went on at Willie Week that year. A particular focus of the video is conversations with and music from four icons of the tradition who have long since passed, singers Tom Lenihan and Nora Cleary and musicians John Kelly Sr. and Junior Crehan. Even though Junior was speaking in English, the producers felt they needed to add subtitles to help Americans understand what he was saying – although I had no trouble with it myself. At one point, the interviewer mentions that Matt Molloy played Junior's tune Poll an Madra Uisce, aka The Otter's Holt, with The Chieftains, to which Junior responds, with typical Irish matter-of-factness, *Matt Molloy. A* good *flute player*.

Although I had thought my mental picture would end up being the only memory I'd ever have of how I danced that evening, in a strange twist of fate about five years later at a dance weekend I met a woman who said I looked like someone she'd seen dancing in a video she had. She described the set I had danced and the plaid shirt I was wearing that night, as well as the hair I'd had then and subsequently lost. I don't know how she ended up with it, but she had a copy of the raw footage from that evening, and she made a copy for me and mailed it to me after she got home. It's nice to have, but frankly my mental picture was better than the videotaped reality. But isn't it always thus?

Following the excitement of the Thursday night dance concert and the relative letdown of class on Friday and Saturday, I headed off to Dublin for the last few days of my holiday in Ireland. I wanted to go to a pub called The Merchant, where I'd heard they danced sets on Saturday nights. I checked into my B&B, which was well north of the River Liffey near the airport, and set off in the car to the pub, which sits across the street from the Brazen Head on the south bank of the river on Merchant's Quay. (The Brazen Head, by the way, is Ireland's oldest pub, dating back about a thousand years, but when I went into it the next day I found it to be in better shape than Nanny O'Brien's in Washington, dating back about thirty years.) Not being familiar with the parking situation in Dublin, I parked well up O'Connell Street and walked over a mile to The Merchant, getting there by around half nine, when I figured the dancing might be starting up. Fortunately for me this was in the long twilight of an Irish summer evening, because I later found out that if I'd made that walk after dark I probably would have gotten mugged. I think the same kind Irish couple who told me that, and who gave me a ride back to the car at the end of the evening, were also the folks to whom, as we were watching the dancing at The Merchant, I casually mentioned that I had been out in West Clare the previous week trying to learn how to do the dancing myself. I had no intention of dancing that night, but this couple insisted that I must, and went up to the *fear an ti* and pointed out that there was a visitor present who should be dancing. He found me a partner, and the next thing I knew I found myself out on the floor. The kind couple who outed me as a dancer were also considerate enough to snap a few photos and send them along to me later. So now not only can I remember how I once danced in Dublin, I also have a stark reminder of what life was like for a guy with male-pattern baldness in the days before Rogaine or the option to shave your head without being mistaken for a cancer patient.

If this first visit to Ireland twenty years ago left me with nothing else, it left me with the strong urge to go back. Which I have, seven times since, and four of those visits have included a return trip to Willie Week. The pattern emerged for me to build a trip around attending an event like Willie Week or the Feakle Festival and sandwiching touristy things around that. People would say *Who are you traveling with?* and when I'd tell them I was going by myself they'd say *Well then you must have relatives there to visit.* But I didn't, and as I learned from my friend Sue Casey who did have aunts, uncles and cousins in Ireland, that's a *good* thing – because for someone who does have relatives there, if you travel all the way to Ireland and don't stop in to see them, there's hell to pay. That can really eat up your vacation time and keep you from doing all the things you came to Ireland to do in the first place.

In truth, though, I had the best of both worlds, because on several of my trips Joe and Siobhan O'Donovan opened their home in Cork to me for a few days. They were just turning 70 around the time I met them – in fact, the first Cape May Dance Weekend that I helped organize with the Greater Washington Ceili Club in 1988 was a celebration of Joe's 70th birthday – so they were almost like grandparents for me. They lived on the fringe of Cork City in a comfortable house that they'd built right after their wedding and had raised their family in. When they built the house, their townland, called Mayfield, was rather rural, and the city had grown out to meet them over time. But even though there were lots of other houses around them, they had a secluded back garden that Siobhan kept full of flowering bushes. As is typical of Irish houses not located in the inner reaches of big cities, their dwelling did not have a street name and number. Rather, it had a name. *Dun Chaoin*, which Joe told me meant *the quiet fort*. Simply addressing an envelope *Joe and Siobhan O'Donovan, Dun Chaoin, Mayfield, Co. Cork, Ireland* was enough to get it there – provided you could figure out how much postage to add. That was the real trick.

There certainly was no guarantee if I showed up in Ireland that Joe and Siobhan would take me in. They weren't real relatives, so they didn't *have* to, the way real relatives would. And I was far from the only one who rated the privilege, since the O'Donovans were masters at acquiring friends. They only made three or four trips to America before Siobhan's fear of flying took hold, but there were at least a couple of people from every place they'd visited who they had begun corresponding with. So at any given time, especially during the summer, there might be several folks touring around Ireland and hoping to spend a couple of nights in Dun Chaoin. And there *was* a pecking order. Jim Burns from Baltimore got priority over me, even though he had quit dancing years before and I was still mad for it myself. But Jim absolutely doted on Joe and Siobhan, much more than I ever could have, so that was okay. If we both happened to be over in the same year for Willie Week, he'd go to Cork beforehand and I'd go after, or the other way around.

And so it was that I got to spend several two- or three-day chunks of my vacations at the O'Donovan house. All the amenities (and more) of a B&B, with none of the cost. Looking back, I do have to admit that I perhaps took advantage of the situation. Fueled by one of Siobhan's massive morning fry-ups I would head out on a tourist jaunt, returning late in the afternoon just in time for dinner. I toured Cork City, went to the emigration harbor town of Cobh, climbed Blarney Castle, and even drove 100 miles from there to Kilkenny one day just to tour the Smithwick's Brewery. (I had developed an obsession with Smithwick's on one of my first trips to Ireland, and its mystique was only heightened by the fact that it wasn't then available in America. Now that it is, I'm more likely to order a Guinness. Go figure.) While I was out, Joe made recordings for me of some classic vinyl albums, using a machine he had that included a turntable and a cassette recorder all in one. He neatly wrote out all the tune names on the cassette sleeves. Siobhan would do my laundry, if I was at the end of my trip, so I wouldn't have to fly home with a suitcase full of dirty clothes. I did pay a price for that service, though, because I'd come back to the sight of my boxers flying in the wind on the clothesline in their back garden.

In the evenings, if there was a dance event or a session somewhere near Cork, Joe would take me out to it and I would have instant entrée thanks to his reputation among dancers and musicians alike. I got to sit in on a small session with Seamus Creagh and a few others when I was barely beyond being a beginner flute player. If it was a ceili or dance class we were at, Joe (and Siobhan, who was usually along) would make sure I never wanted for a good dance partner. But there were many evenings where we didn't venture out at all, but instead would sit around the dining room table late into the night talking and drinking Paddy, the whiskey from Cork. I recall one such night when Joe and I finished off pretty much a whole bottle of it, with Joe leading the way – although I did do my share. Joe had spent his working life as an engineer traveling around Ireland to various job sites, and while he was there he would absorb the local nuances of step dancing, set dancing, music and culture – this being a time when there actually *were* local nuances to be absorbed, the great homogenization of Irish traditional culture not having yet occurred. And Joe's own roots in the tradition were deep indeed, as his father was a dancing master before him and taught him steps that dated back to the first half of the 19th century. Thankfully these steps are in no danger of being lost, since younger dancers flocked to Joe during his later years to learn the old hornpipe steps and other *sean nos* steps from him. Regan Wick, who used to live in Washington, learned them from Joe at the Augusta Irish Week and then danced them on stage with the band Celtic Thunder. Kieran Jordan of Boston went over to Ireland to study with Joe, and now travels all over performing and teaching the steps, as well as nurturing a whole network of women doing *sean nos* dancing that includes my friend Shannon Dunne who lives just outside DC. The greatest exponent of Joe's style of dance is a fellow called Patrick

O'Dea who I first saw dancing in the 1990s at Willie Week when he was barely a teenager. Although he lived then in England with his family, he came over to Ireland often to study with Joe. Even at that young age, on stage dancing the steps he was a virtual clone of Joe. Now, two decades later, he travels the same paths Joe once did and teaches at festivals and workshops as Joe once did – making him the third generation of a tree of dancing masters that began with Joe's father over 100 years ago. The tradition endures.

Although I tried a few times, I never did learn any dances from Joe other than the Caledonian, Plain, Kerry and other sets that we danced at the ceilis. No old hornpipe steps with the names of some 19th century dancing master on them, no *sean nos* steps. I ended up playing the music, not dancing to it. But still, what I learned from Joe either around his dining room table or on dance floors from Glen Echo to Cape May to Miltown Malbay permeates my approach to the music. Although I appreciate and love listening to the innovative take on traditional music that the best players of the new young generation are putting out there, if my own playing is influenced by anything (and I hope it is) and if there is anyone I try to emulate, it will be the player in the old traditional style. From Joe's example, I can see that the old styles can constantly be made fresh and new and carry one through a long life in the tradition. And I cannot summon memories of Joe O'Donovan without also thinking of his wife Siobhan, who was always by his side. After all, it was she who pulled me out of the crowd of dancers on the floor in the Community Hall to be part of the group to dance on stage at Willie Week in 1987. Otherwise, I would never have gotten to know them as I did. Siobhan always told the story of how she started dancing the steps when she was already past 50 years old. She was at a party with Joe and someone asked them to dance a few steps. She protested to Joe that she didn't know any of the steps he danced, and he said *Ah, you can just dance the threes and sevens.* (Those are the first steps learned by a beginning ceili dancer.) *This crowd is so drunk they won't know the difference.* So she did, and found herself hooked. She went on to learn the steps and dance alongside Joe for the rest of his life. And of course, even though Joe was the far better dancer, she always got the biggest round of applause. Siobhan O'Donovan is my patron saint of coming to the tradition later in life.

The last couple of times I was in Ireland, in the early 2000s, my travels did not take me to Cork. Had I gone there I would not have stayed with the O'Donovans anyway, because it would have been too much of a burden on them. They still lived together in the house called Dun Chaoin, but as they approached 90 years old their lives were taken up by caring for each other, seemingly alternating turns as first one, then the other, experienced a medical issue. I was able to talk with them on the phone once or twice while I was in Ireland, and I heard through the grapevine that Joe had retired from teaching his dance classes, first the one at Willie Week that had given me my own start, and then his weekly class in Cork. Then, one evening in early May 2008 I went out to RiRa pub in Bethesda, where our itinerant local session had settled at the time. I was playing the Rudall and Rose flute that I had bought from Patrick Olwell the summer before, and for several hours all was well. It seemed as if I was playing better than I had in a good long while. Then, all of a sudden, I literally hit the wall. Not only were my fingers and embouchure no longer doing what my brain was telling them to, my brain itself was no longer firing on all cylinders. I had to pack up and head home. I thought at the time that it was probably the combination of a busy week and the two pints of Smithwick's that had put the sudden whammy on me, but now I'm not so sure about that. I'm no big believer in cosmic coincidences, mind you, but I learned the next morning shortly after I logged in that Joe O'Donovan had died over the night.

It had been at least five years since I had seen Joe and Siobhan, but a few weeks before Joe died my heart was warmed and fond memories were raised when TG4, the Irish-language television channel, awarded them one of its Gradam Ceol awards for 2008. Joe was too ill for he and Siobhan to come to the grand hall and receive their award from Irish President Mary MacAleese, but their children were there to accept it for them. As part of the ceremony a marvelous tribute video including a recent interview with Joe and Siobhan was aired. Although slowed by age, the Joe and Siobhan I had first met at Willie Week in 1987 were clearly still present, and it was wonderful to experience their presence – even if only via a TG4 video – one last time. I hope that video remains out there for all those readers who were not fortunate enough to have met Joe and Siobhan O'Donovan themselves, so they can watch it and see who they were. If a picture is worth a thousand words, this video is worth much more than these thousands of mine.

When Joe O'Donovan died, those of us who knew him said that it would be impossible to think of Siobhan living on without her beloved Joe. Yet it was almost five years later that she slipped gently away at almost 95 years of age. In another cosmic coincidence, I learned of her death first thing in the morning after I'd decided to add a little more about them in this chapter as I was doing the final editing of this book.

*Joe and Siobhan O'Donovan dancing in O'Shea's Hotel, Dublin, January 1990.*

# The Dublin Porter

Whenever something establishes itself as The One True Path, rarely is there just one prophet or one guru for it, and the introduction and subsequent obsession with Irish set dancing in the Washington area was no exception to this. In the early 1980s Michael Denney was teaching ceili dancing in Washington and Baltimore. His pedigree was strong, as he learned his dancing as a youth from Peggy O'Neill, widely acknowledged as the godmother of Irish dancing in Washington, and his parents were the co-founders of the Blackthorn Stick, the standard-bearers of the *Ar Rince Foirne* ceili dances, both in performance and socially at their monthly ceili. But one time while he was on a spree over in Ireland, Michael stumbled across a group doing something called the Kerry Set. It was danced to polkas and slides, two rhythms virtually unheard of in ceili dancing. And the footwork was not the predictable threes-and-sevens of ceili dancing, but instead a percussive step that was much lower to the floor, with the heel of the foot playing the lead instead of the ceili dancer's toes. Immediately hooked, Michael came home with the figures of the set written on the back of an envelope and began teaching it – even though he knew he didn't have it quite "right" yet. But that didn't matter, because he taught it as if he did.

Around the same time, Paul Keating – a New Yorker with Clare roots who had been teaching ceili dancing in New York – made the same journey that I myself made a few years later. He went to the Willie Clancy Summer School, where he took the beginner set dancing class with Joe and Siobhan O'Donovan. He came home evangelized and began teaching the sets himself, primarily the North Kerry Set (which was then just called the Kerry Set, no other sets from Kerry having yet been revived) and the Caledonian Set, which were the two sets that spearheaded the great revival of Irish country set dancing. Somewhere along the way, Paul and Michael networked, which resulted in Michael meeting the O'Donovans and learning and eventually teaching the Caledonian Set himself. Terry Winch once wrote a poem about Mike Denney that started off *Michael Denney likes to talk about dancing / Even more than he likes to dance* – and Michael Denney was a *great* dancer. It only stands to reason that all his talking about dancing would have impact as well, and so it was that the Greater Washington Ceili Club was formed to promote set dancing in the greater Washington, D.C. area and to run an Irish Festival at Glen Echo Park, not always in that order of importance. This is where I joined the story, walking into the Spanish Ballroom at Glen Echo Park one Wednesday evening in the spring of 1987 to take a class in Irish set dancing taught by Mike Denney. By July of that year I was in Miltown Malbay dancing the Kerry Set under the aegis of Joe and Siobhan O'Donovan.

But I was soon to discover that there was another branch to the set dancing tree. Diana Jensen, who was the founding president of the GWCC, and her husband Ron had gone to a literary week in County Clare where, to loosen things up in the midst of all the academic goings-on, there was a lunchtime class in set dancing every day. The class was taught by an enthusiastic, energetic, bearded and burly County Tipperary man called Connie Ryan, who worked as a telephone switchboard operator in Dublin by day and spent every other waking moment (and possibly much of the time he was asleep) as an evangelist of Irish set dancing. Diana and Ron quickly fell under his spell, and before long arrangements were made with the assistance of Paul Keating to bring Connie Ryan and a troupe of some 56 dancers and musicians over from Ireland for a tour in America. They called themselves the Slievenamon Set Dancing Club; Slievenamon (*Sliabh na mBan* in Irish, literally "the mountain of the women") being a well-known landmark in Connie Ryan's native county. This name gave them the rights to use a well known waltz-time song as their theme song throughout the tour.

*Alone all alone by the wave-washed strand*
*And alone in a crowded hall*
*The hall it is gay and the waves they are grand*
*But my heart is not here at all*
*It lies far away by night and by day*
*To the times and the joys that are gone*
*But I never will forget the sweet maiden I met*
*In the valley near Slievenamon*

Aside from Connie Ryan himself and Dick Hogan, the man who sang this song – every hour on the hour, it seemed, but that was okay – I don't think any of the others in the group were from Tipp, so they may well never even have been near Slievenamon, much less in the thrall of any of its local maidens. The group's musical director was a Clare man, Michael Tubridy, late of The Chieftains, and it seemed that most of the rest of them were from Dublin. But their widespread origin didn't matter a whit, because they operated like a well-oiled machine. Only later did I discover that this Slievenamon Set Dancing Club was not some long-standing institution, but rather a group that was put together specifically for the purposes of this tour. It was their maiden voyage.

They started at the Glen Echo Irish Festival, then in its third year of GWCC sponsorship, performing in the afternoon under the festival tents and running the festival ceili in the Spanish Ballroom in the evening. Later in the week the musicians from the group did their musical numbers on the postage-stamp stage in The Dubliner pub, and the next weekend the entire group reprised their festival performance in Baltimore and followed it with a ceili. Then the Slievenamon group left Charm City on its way home to Ireland, leaving us Washington-Baltimore set dancers thoroughly exhilarated, yet chastened by what was, for many of us, our first exposure to "the real thing." We realized we had a lot to learn, and the only way to learn it would be to go to the source. So plans were hatched to do just that.

On Wednesday evening, January 10th, 1990, a British Airways jet took off from Dulles Airport carrying some fifty members, friends and general hangers-on of the Greater Washington Ceili Club. Destination: Dublin, with a brief stop to change planes in Heathrow. We were paying a return visit to Connie Ryan and the Slievenamon Set Dancing Club. The party started almost as soon as our flight left the ground, thanks to British Air's free drinks policy. One of our party was so excited that he was practicing his steps in the aisle of the plane at 30,000 feet. (No, it wasn't me.) We landed in Dublin on Thursday afternoon, hopped onto a bus and headed straight for the pub. There were two reasons for this. First, it was the pub. But mainly, it was because our hotel accommodations weren't quite ready for us yet.

The Slievenamon group had arranged for us to stay in a hotel on Talbot Street, a few blocks north of the River Liffey behind the Custom House. The premises had been known as Moran's Hotel, but it had recently been bought by Ned O'Shea, one of the musicians who traveled with the Slievenamon group and also the owner of The Merchant Pub, the premier venue for set dancing in Dublin. Our group of dancers were to be the first guests in the newly-refurbished O'Shea's Hotel, but although we had booked the trip months in advance apparently they had waited until the very last minute to undertake the renovations. A round-the-clock marathon of work was not quite done as we arrived. Nails were still being pounded and carpet was still being laid. But the pub was up and running, so there we went to wait it out.

Our group of dancers would not be doing any performances or running any ceilis while we were in Dublin, but we still thought it would be a good idea if we brought a "staff musician" with us, so we hired Brendan Mulvihill and brought him along for the week. Although the offer of an all-expenses-paid trip to Dublin where all he had to do was play the fiddle was quite appealing, as it turned out we were really putting Brendan to the test. He was off the drink at the time, and here we were taking him right into the belly of the beast. Our trip to the pub upon arrival challenged him immediately. Suzanne McMenamin saddled up to the bar and ordered a pint of Guinness, the Dublin Porter at its very source. Brendan was right behind her, eyes wide and nostrils flared. But he held strong. *Ooooh, oooh, Suzanne, can I sniff your pint? All I want is to sniff your pint.* The sweet aroma of Guinness was apparently enough to last him the week. It helped that he was using tea to substitute for the drink, and in Dublin we were surrounded by shops filled with the finest tea money could buy. Brendan traveled light that week. He had only two small bags and his fiddle with him. But when I saw him in the hotel lobby the morning we were headed home, one of those bags was entirely filled with boxes of tea.

In due time everything got sorted out and our lodgings were made available to us. It turned out that I had been booked to share a room with three other guys, Barry Stohlman, George Kuhn and Ken Hager. Normally this would not have been an issue, but when we lugged our bags up to the second floor, went down the hall and unlocked the door we discovered that the room was the size of a closet and had only two double beds. Now, Barry, George and Ken are all nice guys, but they are also all bigger than me. I couldn't picture myself spending a week fighting for bed space with any of them, so I immediately headed across the street to a guest house I'd noticed earlier and booked myself into a room there. It was small, up several flights of stairs with no elevator available, and had the bathroom down the hall. But it did offer a private bed for those few hours every day when I'd be looking for some peace, quiet and sleep. And I could still go across the street to O'Shea's and eat the breakfast there in the morning.

The guest house also featured its own Dublin Porter, but not the kind you drink. As it happened, I found myself spending much of that week squiring around one of the lady dancers from our group. One evening after dinner we were looking to get away from the rest of the group and the tight quarters of O'Shea's Hotel. As we walked into the guest house to head up the stairs to my room, we were intercepted by the porter at the front desk. *No visitors allowed, sir.* This seemed strange to me, because never before or since at a B&B in Ireland did anyone care if someone came to visit me in my room. But this same man had thought I was Irish when I checked in (I guess I didn't say enough for him to pick up on my obvious American accent) and perhaps this place was known for local men booking rooms for nefarious purposes. Whatever the reason, my friend and I were exiled back over to O'Shea's, where we made do. This carried on for the rest of the week, until the last night arrived – which happened to be your man's night off. With no one manning the front desk, we just waltzed right up to my room. Timing is everything.

As it turns out, timing is also everything when trying to catch some daylight in Dublin in January. If you blink, you miss it. In contrast to – or maybe it's payback for – the long summer evenings of light in Ireland, in January it gets dark around 4:00 in the afternoon. I have no idea what time the sun comes up there in winter, except that it's earlier than the noon timeframe we were forcing the providers of our daily breakfast to adhere to. In other words, we saw the sun four hours out of every day while we were there – on those days that it wasn't overcast, that is. Which means we hardly saw the sun at all for an entire week. But that didn't matter, because we came to Dublin to dance the sets, and dance the sets we did. (Okay, we did also drink more than a few pints of the Dublin Porter, and Smithwick's too.) We attended Connie Ryan's regular Thursday night dance class at the Ierne Ballroom in Parnell Square on the day we arrived. There were more sets of dancers there than we'd have at the largest ceili of the year at home, which was always the Irish Festival ceili in Glen Echo's Spanish Ballroom. But the Ierne Ballroom was smaller than that, which meant that us Yanks were all crowded in the back, barely able to see what Connie's demonstration set was doing up front. And for the most part, the Irish dancers kept to their regular partners rather than reaching out to us visitors, but really, who could blame them? When it came to dance acumen, most of us had arrived on the short bus, nowhere near being ready for the postgraduate seminar that Connie was conducting there that night. But still, we had a grand time, and learning happened as if by osmosis. As it is with real estate, all that matters is location, location, location. One's Irish dancing skills are always better when the steps are done in Ireland.

Steps of the Clare and Kerry sets were trod by us in all the O'Shea premises in Dublin. On Friday night we visited The Merchant for an evening of dancing. This was the same pub that I had visited on the tail end of my first trip to Ireland a few years before. That night, upon realizing they had a Yank in their midst who was learning the dancing, the organizers had practically forced me onto the floor, fixing me up with a partner and everything. The *Cead Mile Fealte* for our large group was not quite the same. Again, we spent most of the evening dancing with ourselves. This cemented a truth I had learned early on: wherever possible, break free of the tour group. (If only the bands of beginners and bodhran players who descend on sessions expecting to be welcomed with open arms could figure this out.)

But I don't want to give the impression that our Irish hosts were totally unwelcoming. They arranged a reception for us at the Mansion House, where all of us had the chance to watch as our leaders, Diana Jensen and Mike Denney, were presented to the Lord Mayor of Dublin himself by Connie Ryan. The Mansion House being one of those places that boasts a great floor for dancing but lives in mortal fear that people might actually dance on it and scuff it up, only a brief demonstration figure from a single set was allowed to be danced in front of the esteemed Lord Mayor, decked out in his ceremonial necklace. But it did at least give us the chance to show that we weren't a total bunch of rubes, and that maybe we might be catching onto this set dancing thing after all.

Fortunately O'Shea's Hotel featured a ballroom with a great dance floor, and they didn't mind if people actually danced on it. Two massive ceilis were arranged for the weekend in honor of our visit. Joe and Siobhan O'Donovan, who had become friends of GWCC thanks to their appearances at the Glen Echo Irish Festival in 1986 and the inaugural Cape May Ceili Weekend in 1988, came up from Cork to join us at one of the ceilis. (Actually, they had children and grandchildren living in Dublin, so that may have played a part in their visit as well.) The dance floor in O'Shea's was packed out for the entirety of both ceilis, along with the bar that sat on a raised level in the back. If you stood at the bar while a set was being danced, you could watch the dancers on the floor sway up and down like the waves on the sea. This was not because they were correctly dancing the Clare step (although they were) but because the floor was so well sprung. Aside from learning how the steps and figures of the Clare and Kerry sets were *supposed* to be done, we learned as well that a true ceili was not the genteel sort of event we were putting on in Washington. As soon as Connie Ryan would announce the next set, the words barely out of his mouth, dozens of sets of eight dancers would fill the floor as if by magic. Staking one's turf on the dance floor was paramount. No announcements from the stage of *Need one couple to fill out that set in the back* or anything of the sort. We Yanks quickly adapted to this and would have our set ready to hit the floor, not caring what set was being called next. Whatever it was, we'd muddle through it. We'd charge out there and claim a chunk of dance floor, standing in formation so as to maintain some breathing room around us to do the round the houses and the houses at home. But always, without fail, as soon as the first note would sound our set would be squeezed into the smallest possible chunk of floor by the Irish sets around us. It was pretty clear whose home it was that we were housing around.

But there was one place where our hosts treated us as equals: the bar. Although there may have been an ulterior motive at play here. The Irish licensing laws allow for a hotel bar to remain open as long as there are residents wanting to be served, no matter how late in the night it gets. So our host dancers did everything they could to keep us all up and drinking in the bar in O'Shea's, so they could join us. Black plastic sheets were placed over the windows, just in case some *garda* who was a stickler for the rules might happen by during the night. The Dublin Porter flowed freely, and the *craic* was mighty every night until dawn. Or almost until dawn, anyway, dawn coming so late in the day of an Irish winter. Eventually, we visiting Yanks would crawl up to bed, but our Dublin hosts had other things to do. Even though this was several years before the Celtic Tiger began to roar, these folks all had day jobs. While we slept until noon, they would put in a day at the office and then join us the next night to do it all again. The last night, with our bus to the airport scheduled to leave before sunrise, we dispensed with sleep ourselves and partied all night. As the bus pulled away from the hotel in the morning, flakes of snow falling, there were the Dublin dancers of Slievenamon on the front steps, waving goodbye to us. We were all knackered, ready to sleep it off on the flight home. They were headed off to work. How did they possibly do it? I think one of those posters I saw all over Ireland was right. Guinness for Strength. The Dublin Porter at its very source is a magical thing. Even a mere sniff of it can do wonders.

# The Festival: Glen Echo Years

On Memorial Day Weekend in 1985, I went to Glen Echo Park for an Irish music festival I had heard about. I'd been to Glen Echo a couple of times before then for something called the Washington Folk Festival, where bands of local "folkies" performed mainly for each other over the course of a weekend in tents set up on the Glen Echo grounds. Glen Echo was at that time a run-down former amusement park that had closed down after its segregationist policies caused controversy in the 1960s. It was reborn as a National Park Service site, mainly for the purpose of keeping it out of the hands of nasty real estate developers who would ruin the neighborhood. It was a rather picturesque site, if you could ignore the run-down buildings scattered about. The Park Service put only enough resources into the place to keep it from falling apart, which made it an ideal venue for groups that had no money to stage events like the Washington Folk Festival and the Irish Festival I had wandered into. I wasn't too impressed with the Irish Festival in 1985. They only had a couple of stages set up, one in the shell of the old bumper car ride and the other in something called the Cuddle Up. No big white tents like the Washington Folk Festival had. I only stayed at the Irish Festival for a few hours, even though as I recall it was a nice sunny spring day. But this little festival did make enough of an impression on me to get me to come back the next year.

Something was clearly different at the Glen Echo Irish Festival in 1986. More stages – including a couple of big white tents. More bands performing. A much bigger crowd. I later learned that this was the first year that the Greater Washington Ceili Club ran the festival. Only recently formed as a group to promote Irish set dancing, they had jumped at an opportunity to bid on the right to operate this festival, which had been going on since 1977, when there was lots of government grant money flowing for ethnic and folk arts events in the wake of the 1976 Bicentennial. Those government grants had apparently led to two or three years of a very impressive Memorial Day weekend festival at Glen Echo, with lots of performers brought in from Ireland and from U.S. cities with lots of Irish emigrants. In other words, the real thing. But then the grant money ran out and the festival carried on as a sort of block party for locals who played Irish music or sang Irish songs, with no real concern about authenticity.

I soon found myself a member of that Greater Washington Ceili Club, after seeing Irish set dancing at the Augusta Irish Week and deciding that I wanted to learn how to do it myself. At the first dance class I attended at Glen Echo's Spanish Ballroom, I learned that the teacher, Mike Denney, was also the director of the Glen Echo Irish Festival. Being that the festival was an all-volunteer event, a major component of the dance class was a push to gather volunteers for the festival. I got sucked into this, and little did I know then what I was getting myself into.

The 1987 festival was my first as a volunteer. I believe one of my duties was to man the door at the Spanish Ballroom during the ceili and enforce the Park Service's no-alcohol policy. The primary qualification for this job was the inability to recognize a cooler full of beer as it was carried into the ballroom right under one's nose. I managed to do this, and got a few dances in for myself to boot. The park rangers at Glen Echo, when it came to enforcing the no-alcohol policy, did Sgt. Schultz of Hogan's Heroes one better. They knew *less* than nothing. They didn't even know that in addition to providing pizza for the festival performers, the festival hospitality crew provided beer – by strategically "abandoning" a cooler full of it out in the picnic area. Thus every performer's second question upon checking in at the festival site was always *What time do I go on?* Their first question was *Where's the beer?* Sometimes after getting an answer to the first question, they didn't even bother with the second question. I learned early on that rule number one of festival organizing was to always know where your performers were. This would serve me in good stead for years to come, hastening my rise to bigger and better positions in the festival hierarchy.

One of the reasons the Irish Festival suddenly got better when the GWCC took over was that they entered into a strategic partnership with the Folklore Society of Greater Washington, who produced the Washington Folk Festival that took place the weekend after the Memorial Day weekend Irish Festival. This meant that the Irish Festival got to use the same tents and stages that the Folk Festival used, with the condition that they provide slave labor to help set them up, as well as performing other general maintenance work around the park. It seemed that the Folk Festival's Technical Director Dwain Winters had a secret agenda of rebuilding Glen Echo Park bit by bit because the National Park Service wasn't going to do it. So it was that I soon found myself doing tasks at the park that I otherwise wouldn't be doing even in my own home – things like painting, crawling underneath buildings to help shore up their foundation, scrubbing the rust off things, general cleaning, sweeping up and the like. I've never been a big fan of manual labor, so perhaps it was this experience that spurred me into taking more of a desk job as the Volunteer Coordinator for the 1989 festival.

Dwain Winters had a motley crew of acolytes who collectively were known as Festival Operations. They specialized in creating the infrastructure for the two festivals virtually from scratch each May, building it piece by piece over the course of several so-called Work Weekends at the Park. (An oxymoron if there ever was one.) These were the folks who we Irish Festival types took our direction from. *Move this. Stand there and hold this in place. Hook this up to that.* Why? We never knew. Then as the first of the two festivals approached, a giant work crew of volunteers was needed to erect the tents. Since we were operating with the same level of technology as had been used to erect the Egyptian Pyramids, the process of erecting just one tent took hours – a job that a couple of beefy guys with cranes and forklifts could do in a matter of minutes for the circus. On festival day, Operations would swarm around the park with walkie talkies in hand, or drive golf carts around, as they put out fires – figuratively, not literally, although secretly they all wished they could have a *real* fire to put out – and ensured that everything went smoothly. As soon as the last note was sounded on the Sunday of the Washington Folk Festival, this same Operations crew, augmented by navvies from the Irish Festival, would tear everything down and hide it all away, so that the next morning there would be no evidence that the festivals ever happened. Kind of like Brigadoon, without the corny show tunes.

As essential as the Operations crew was to the success of the festivals, I often had the feeling that they'd be every bit as happy if no performances took place at all while they did their thing. For them, the music didn't seem to matter. But it did to me. Indeed that was the reason I was there in the first place. So in what seemed to me a natural progression, after a couple of years of involvement with the festival I found myself on the committee that put the program together. We called it the Entertainment Committee. That's where things got *really* interesting.

When the Ceili Club took over the Irish Festival in 1986, it started changes on two fronts: production values and quality of performance. No one had any complaint with the improvements in production values. Everyone, performers and audiences alike, likes better stages, bigger tents, nicer sound systems and the like. But as the Ceili Club – in the person of Festival Director Mike Denney – sought to change the list of performers who got to appear on those nicer stages in front of bigger audiences, serious conflicts emerged. In many cases, long held grudges got to play themselves out yet again.

The Glen Echo Irish Festival as it had evolved by 1985 featured a lineup of entirely local performers. I'm not sure about this, but I doubt any of them were being paid to play their set of tunes or songs at the festival. These were the same ballad singers and bands who played every night of the week in the many Irish pubs around town. The festival was a nice picnic afternoon in the park for them, a chance for them to gain some exposure and maybe find some new patrons to come out for their bar gigs. After six or seven years of this, they'd become used to it, perhaps even taking it for granted. And when the Ceili Club started to change things, the changes happened gradually and perhaps they didn't pick up on what was happening. But eventually they did.

The first big addition to the Irish Festival lineup that Mike Denney engineered was in 1986, when in cooperation with Paul Keating in New York he brought Joe and Siobhan O'Donovan over from Cork to teach set dancing workshops in the afternoon and to run the Festival Ceili in the Spanish Ballroom that capped the event on Sunday night. This was completely in line with the Ceili Club's mission to promote set dancing, and it didn't displace any of the previous regular performers, so of course there was no objection from anyone. The 1986 Glen Echo Irish Festival was an unqualified success, which fed the fire for bigger and better things in years to come.

Glen Echo Park would not allow an admission fee to be charged for the Irish Festival or for the Washington Folk Festival that took place a week later. That was something I never understood, because they allowed admission fees to be charged for contradances, carousel rides and other events at the park. But such were the archaic rules of the National Park Service, and the net result was that for the festivals money was always a problem. The Folk Festival dealt with that by not paying its performers, which kept it as a purely local event. Mike Denney's vision for the Irish Festival was bigger than that, and money was needed to support that vision. The Park Service would allow advertisements to be sold, so ads were sold for the festival program book, which the Park service would not allow us to sell. Again, go figure. But they would allow us to raise a banner behind a stage with the name of a "sponsor", so several thousand dollars were raised by selling stage sponsorships to the likes of Coca-Cola. Bob Hickey was a main man in pulling in sponsorship money, which in future years would reveal itself to be a mixed blessing.

The extra money raised in 1987 allowed several "traditional" or "authentic" Irish musicians to be brought in from New York and Boston to perform alongside the locals. These imports were primarily tune players rather than singers, and they were all either first or second generation Irish immigrants who had started learning their music in childhood. As it happened, at that time in the Washington-Baltimore area there were quite a few recent Irish immigrants in the ballad-singing bar bands, but not as many "authentic" musicians playing Irish tunes. Brendan Mulvihill and Billy McComiskey, who had come to DC from New York in the late 1970s as part of the band The Irish Tradition, and Jesse and Terry Winch, who moved from New York to DC around the same time and formed the band Celtic Thunder, were about it. But in their decade or so in Washington, these two groups had fostered a dedicated coterie of players who had taken up Irish dance music as adults. Some of them were quite good at it, too. But none of them were "traditional" or "authentic." That didn't matter, though, as they enjoyed the opportunity to meet and play alongside the likes of Joe Burke and Michael Cooney, Seamus Connolly, James Keane, Seamus Egan (then but 17 years old), Eileen Ivers, John Whelan, Robbie O'Connell and Tommy Sands at the 1987 festival. That year also saw the debut of Cape Breton fiddle music at the festival, in the person of Jerry Holland, Dave MacIsaac and Hilda Chiasson. This came thanks to family connections Mike Denney had on Cape Breton, an island off the coast of Nova Scotia in Canada. The music wasn't Irish, it was Scottish. But it was as "traditional" and "authentic" as you could get. And it was *great* music.

Many of these musicians came back for the 1988 festival, which also featured the visiting Slievenamon Set Dancing Club from Ireland, headed up by dance master Connie Ryan, sadly now gone, who went on to shepherd the GWCC's Cape May Set Dancing Weekend that is now named in memory of him. The Slievenamon Ceili Band featured some 20 musicians including former Chieftain Michael Tubridy, and a full complement of dancers. Michael's wife Celine dancing The Priest in his Boots set dance to his whistle accompaniment was a highlight of the Slievenamon performance. The irrepressible Joanie Madden also made her festival debut that year, accompanied by Mary Coogan. They would be back many times in years to come with the full Cherish the Ladies experience.

The 1989 Festival took place barely three weeks after the parking lot at Glen Echo collapsed during a heavy rainstorm and flood. I was actually there at Glen Echo the night the parking lot collapsed, at a contradance in the Spanish Ballroom. Visitors to Glen Echo today are familiar with the entrance to the park from the parking lot via a footbridge high over a heavily wooded creek bed. But prior to 1989, that creek flowed through a culvert underneath the part of the parking lot closest to the park entrance. The parking lot was not paved as it is now, but just a dusty gravel-covered field. It had been raining heavily the whole day, but I was determined to go to the Friday Night Contradance that night. At the time, I was absolutely obsessed with dancing – Irish first of course, but also contra and swing. Most all of the dances took place in Glen Echo's Spanish Ballroom, definitely the best dance floor in DC and perhaps even on the whole East Coast.

I parked my car in the rear of the parking lot, which turned out to be a fortuitous move, since the lot sloped downward toward the park entrance. There was a large and lively crowd at the dance that night; the lot was packed with cars. It was still raining heavily as I went in, and also when I came out of the ballroom at the break to use the bathroom that was in a different building. I looked down the hill at the parking lot and saw that cars in the first few rows were sitting hubcap deep in a pool of water. Although no one realized it yet, branches, leaves and debris had blocked the upstream entrance to the culvert and there was nowhere for the water to go but over the top of the parking lot. I could see that my car was still on dry ground (so to speak, because the rain continued to pour) so I decided to make my break. Other dancers – some of whose cars were already flooded – decided to go down with the ship and the second half of the dance went on as scheduled. I had to go back into the ballroom to gather my stuff, and when I came back out the water was so deep at the front of the lot that the cars there had lost contact with the ground and were now floating and bobbing around. I could see my car up the slope beyond them, and the pool of water hadn't reached it yet.

It took about 15 minutes for me to hike the roundabout route onto MacArthur Boulevard to get into the parking lot from the back. By the time I reached my car the water level was just under the bottom of the door. I was able to open it, carefully get in, take the brake off, then get out again and with the help of some other folks push it up the hill to get it out of the water. Amazingly, it started, and I was able to drive home. I had dodged a bullet, but dozens of others were not so lucky. The part of the parking lot over the culvert eventually failed under the weight of the water above it, and cars were sucked into the now-raging stream. Several of them ended up all the way out in the Potomac River where the culvert emptied. The next day on TV I watched giant cranes pulling mud-covered cars out of the pit.

I think it was that night when I started to sour on contradancing as a means of recreation. But the Irish Festival was just three weeks away, and it *had*  to go on despite the gaping hole between Glen Echo Park and what used to be its parking lot. Thanks to yeoman work by Dwain Winters and Mike Denney, a satellite parking lot with shuttle buses was arranged and the Festival took place right on schedule. Indeed, the satellite parking scheme worked so smoothly that even after the Park Service rebuilt the Glen Echo lot a couple of years later we continued it. The satellite-parked 1989 event featured the Irish Festival debuts of Brian Gaffney and Zan McLeod with Brendan's Voyage, Dave Abe with the Donegal Stones and Mick Moloney's Green Fields of America with Jimmy Keane, Robbie O'Connell, Eileen Ivers, Seamus Egan and Eugene O'Donnell. Accordionist Keith Corrigan came down from Quebec, the Barra MacNeills from Cape Breton, and among the stable of stepdancers including Deirdre Goulding, Regan and Linnane Wick, Liam Harney and Donny Golden was future Riverdance star Jean Butler. The Stepdancing Spectacular was always a highlight in the Spanish Ballroom, and it may have been this year that the park rangers nabbed several people who were trying to scale the outside of the ballroom building to sneak a look into the packed facility through the windows high above the floor. I also recall a crowd of people standing tip-toed on the flimsy table in the back of the ballroom where all the dance flyers were laid out. We're really lucky no one got hurt, because I don't think we had any insurance!

The festival had made great strides in the first three years I was involved with it, but it came at the expense of ever-increasing resentment from the local musicians who were being squeezed out. In the spring of 1990, it all came to a head. Coincidentally, this was shortly after I became a member of the Entertainment Committee, along with Judy Walsh and Mike and Marleen Denney. We were the brain trust who got to decide who would be invited to perform at the Festival. But even though we were a committee and every one of us had input, when push came to shove it was Mike Denney who called the shots. And for the 1990 edition of the festival, he wanted the number of local performers cut to a bare minimum. There were some sound reasons behind this move; it wasn't purely out of animosity. (Although there were some ancient grudges at play that I had no way of knowing about, since I was so new on the scene myself.) The festival had grown increasingly dependent on grant funding from the National Endowment for the Arts, and in order to award grant funding the NEA put heavy emphasis on "traditionality" and "authenticity." They had strict definitions for those words, and they even had a word of shame for any musician who did not fit their definition of "traditional" and "authentic." No matter how well they played, no matter how traditional their style might have been, those people were "revivalists," and nothing would ever change that. "Revivalists" were most decidedly not worthy of having NEA grant money imposed upon them.

Sadly, almost all of our local musicians were tagged with the stigma of being "revivalists." (To illustrate how great was the stigma the professional folklorists put on these folks who only wanted to play or sing traditional music in as traditional a way that they could – purely out of love and respect for the tradition, nothing more – in 1992 when we had one stage act that were "revivalists" the professional folklorist we had hired to introduce the performers at that stage requested that we get someone else to introduce the "revivalist" group. He would gladly introduce every other act on that stage, just not *that* one.) In order to maintain NEA funding for the festival from 1990 and beyond, Mike Denney decreed that we would need to severely limit the number of local performers who got onto the program. Just three or maybe four such groups a year was all we could handle.

This decision set off a firestorm of protest in the Irish music and dance communities of Washington and Baltimore. Several hundred people signed a petition of protest at the Baltimore Ceili. There were several members of the GWCC Board and the Irish Festival Committee who were dead set against the proposal. Bob Hickey and Don Schuirmann were perhaps the most vocal out of what was definitely a sizable minority of dissenters. The arguments of "traditionality" versus "revivalism" meant nothing to them, but the fact was that the festival as Mike Denney envisioned it could not be presented with NEA money alone, nor could the festival divorce itself from GWCC sponsorship since GWCC held the 501(c)(3) non-profit status that was required to get the NEA funding in the first place. But that didn't matter to those in the minority, because if the proponents of a "big" festival decided to just fold up their tents and quit, they would have been happy to revert back to the kind of purely local festival put on in 1986 and before.

There really was no clean way to resolve this dilemma, but in an attempt to smooth things over a "summit meeting" between the Entertainment Committee and members of three of the local bands was arranged in early March at a pub in Bethesda. Mike Denney and I were the Entertainment Committee representatives (I don't remember if it was a committee decision to only send the two of us, or if the other two members decided on their own not to come) and the bands were Sodabread and Ceoltoiri from DC and Reel Time from Baltimore. The meeting was long and largely congenial, but in the end nothing really changed. The musicians did not understand our decision, and we were not going to change it. One exchange I still recall from this meeting over 20 years ago was when Dennis Botzer said *You mean, just because I'm not as good as Brendan Mulvihill I'm not allowed to play at the festival?* and our answer was *Ummm....yes.* After that exchange, it was out there. No one had any doubt what was really going on.

Now, at that meeting I was basically an unknown quantity. I was a dancer and a festival volunteer, but the local bands really didn't know anything about me other than that. I left the meeting figuring that I had probably generated some resentment from these musicians that would last a long time. Five or six years later when I started going to local sessions myself to play, I did so with trepidation because of the resentment I was sure would still be there among the local music community. Imagine my surprise when two of the musicians who were most welcoming to me at the sessions were Karen Ashbrook and particularly Dennis Botzer, who had both been at that summit meeting.

Which side was right in this battle? Both of them, in a way. Many great festivals were produced in the following decade, and the local Irish music scene grew by leaps and bounds even though not many of the local musicians got to play at the festival. But if the Queen of England can now admit that the Brits made some mistakes in Ireland over the years, I can certainly admit that our policies were a mistake and a huge disservice to these many local musicians – most of of whom are still here, still playing, and now my friends and session mates. One big casualty of those policies is the perception outside the DC area of the Washington music scene. The standard of Irish music in Washington today has never been higher, and it is every bit as high as the standard in Baltimore. Yet outside of Washington, at festivals and summer school weeks up and down the East Coast, it often feels like Irish music doesn't exist in Washington. But *everyone* speaks highly of the Baltimore music scene. If a festival or summer school presents a group of musicians some (or even all) of whom are from Washington, they are invariably advertised or introduced as "from Baltimore." The Washington scene is the Rodney Daingerfield of Irish music scenes. It don't get no respect. And I believe that this attitude can be traced directly back to when we started producing an Irish Festival full of bands from everywhere *but* Washington, and drew an audience with a large percentage of folks from out of town. Washington DC put itself on the map with the Irish Festival, but once the festival ended, no one knew there was any Irish music in Washington because the festival wasn't presenting Irish musicians from Washington. Over 20 years after that fateful decision, attitudes may finally be starting to turn thanks to Washingtonians like Mitch Fanning and Shannon Dunne who are doing outstanding work with young musicians and young dancers, bands like Lilt that are making a name for themselves, and other like endeavors. But 20 years is an awful long time for a group of fine musicians to be disrespected or ignored.

Despite all the political battles, the 1990 Glen Echo Irish Festival was a huge success, in every aspect including financially. The 1990 Festival featured the debuts of Diathi Sproule and Liz Carroll in Trian with local favorite Billy McComiskey, James Kelly, Felix Dolan, Jesse Smith, Mike Rafferty, Joe Madden, Jerry Holland, and Martin Connolly with Maureen Glynn. It's sad to realize that four of these great musicians – Mike Rafferty, Jerry Holland, Joe Madden and Maureen Glynn – are no longer with us, as are so many other folks who played and worked at this festival over the years. Jerry and Maureen were taken well before their time, which is particularly sad.

The 1991 Festival was the complete fruition of Mike Denney's vision for the event. Irish music and dance remained the main focus, but we added representative performers from other traditions where Irish or Scots immigrants had a big influence. We always had Cape Breton music at the festival since it was Mike Denney's first love, and in 1991 it was The Rankin Family. From Quebec we had fiddler Jean-Marie

Verret, accordionist Stephane Landry, dancer and bones player Normand Legault and pianist Benoit Legault. Those guys came to party. Indeed, they *were* the party, even though their English was not that great and our French was non-existent. But the music from Quebec is the happiest music I have ever heard. I wonder what they play at funerals? From Appalachian music we had Sheila Adams and Bruce Molsky. I think this was the first year we ran an evening concert on the Crystal Pool Stage right behind the Spanish Ballroom while the ceili was rocking inside at the same time, this year to a return appearance by the Slievenamon Ceili Band. Glen Echo was a happenin' place that night, and afterward we adjourned to the Phoenix Park Hotel on Capitol Hill and partied till dawn. As one of my volunteer duties I used to drive the performers to the airport to catch their flights home, and there was always more than one who needed to be rousted out of bed at the last possible moment Monday morning to go to the airport, having only bedded down for the night an hour or so before.

First-timers at the Festival in 1991 included Danny Noveck (playing with John Whelan's band), John Williams, Patrick Ourceau and Kieran O'Hare (playing with Dave Abe, Zan McLeod and Myron Bretholz as Skellig).

The 1992 Festival began in turmoil some nine months before the date, when Mike Denney announced that he was burned out and wouldn't be Festival Director any more. Perhaps foolishly, I stepped up and offered to be the director, with Linda Mason and Kathy O'Rourke as co-directors. Of course, Mike Denney did still keep the reins of the Entertainment Committee, which was the ultimate power behind the event. But as the nominal director, I basked in a lot of glory – getting interviewed by Earle Hitchner of the Irish Voice and by some Irish radio journalist (I have no idea if it ever aired) and being the man to greet the Irish ambassador and his wife when they arrived at Glen Echo. I also did a boatload of work – much of it from the premises of my day job. In those pre-voicemail, pre-cellphone days my boss's secretary ended up on a first name basis with vendors, program book advertisers, musicians, bus drivers, and also Mike Denney, who by the end couldn't resist jumping in to do what he'd always done before – which was most welcome and much needed assistance from my overworked perspective. About two days before the festival, my boss finally caught on to what I'd been up to the past three months. He saw me in the hall and said *I hear you're running some festival*. I said *Yeah, but it will all be over Sunday* and kept on walking. Never heard another word about it, and it was another four years before the company laid me off, so I doubt my Irish Festival work had anything to do with that.

## SCHEDULE of EVENTS

| | YURT VILLAGE<br>Stage 1 | SPANISH BALLROOM<br>Stage 2 | CUDDLE UP<br>Stage 3 | CRYSTAL POOL<br>Stage 4 |
|---|---|---|---|---|
| 1:00 | Claddagh | Blackthorn Stick Dancers | Round Stone with Tommy Reilly | Jim Reilly |
| 1:30 | The Irish Breakdown | Joe & Siobhán O'Donovan | Finistère: Breton music | Fire Fighters Emerald Society Pipe Band |
| 2:00 | | Regan & Linnane Wick (O'Hare School) | | |
| 2:30 | Sweet Potatoes | | Pat & Willom Garvey | The Dogs Among the Bushes |
| | | Pauline Malone School | | |
| 3:00 | Chris Norman & Ken Kolodner with Dominick Murray | Brian Gegan — Stepdance 1986 World Champion | Paul Levitt, Uilleann pipes with Philippe Varlet, fiddle | Seamus Kennedy |
| 3:30 | Brendan Mulvihill & Donna Long with The O'Donovans | The Erin Dancers | Crooked Jack | Celtic Thunder with Regan & Linnane Wick |
| 4:00 | | Joe & Siobhán O'Donovan | John Barry, stand-up shanachie | |
| 4:30 | Reel Time with Brian Grant | The O'Neill-James School | Andy O'Brien | Liam Maguire with Fergus Kennedy |
| 5:00 | The Irish Edge with Bill Whitman | Roisin Dubh Dancers | The Mighty Possums | The Erin Senior Dancers |
| 5:30 | | The Greater Washington Céilí Club/workshop | Ceoltoirí | The Shamrock Céilí Band with Mark Quinn |
| 6:00 | Soda Bread | 7:30-11:30 PM CÉILÍ Admission $3 Children (under 13) FREE | Barbara Ryan & Barbara Kelly | |
| 6:30 | Amhranai na nGael/ The Men's Chorus | | | |
| | Stage Manager<br>George Lewett | Stage Manager<br>Mike Kevany | Stage Manager<br>Jim Owens | Stage Manager<br>George Denney |

The Greater Washington Céilí Club in cooperation with The National Park Service presents the annual

## Glen Echo
# IRISH FOLK FESTIVAL
SUNDAY, MAY 25th, 1986

The 1986 Glen Echo Irish Folk Festival program book, such as it was. Design by Susan Campbell.

*Photo by Pat Cady*

Performers at the 1986 Festival included (L—R) Regan Wick, Joe & Siobhan O'Donovan, Linanne Wick & Brian Grant.

Joe O'Donovan always said that he remembered seeing me dancing among the 20+ sets on the floor at the ceili in the Spanish Ballroom that concluded the 1986 Festival. But he didn't, because although I might have been in the room I wasn't dancing yet. I didn't meet Joe and Siobhan until the Willie Clancy Week in July 1987.

Pat Cady was an older Irish gentleman who went to Irish events around town and photographed them gratis under the name The Irish Eye. Every year after the Festival he would present an album of photos to Mike Denney. Pat died sometime in the mid 1990s.

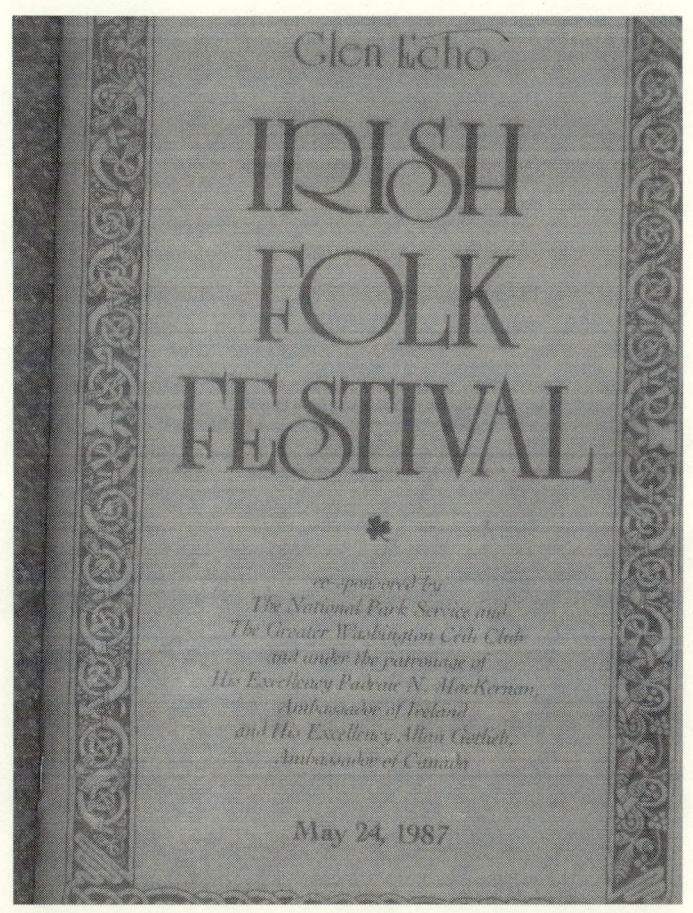

The 1987 Festival was the first of the GWCC-run festivals to feature a significant presence of out-of-town performers. Program book cover design was by Susan Campbell.

The 1988 Festival featured Susan Campbell's iconic fiddle design for the first time, as shown on this poster that I still have framed on the wall in my house. We milked that design for three or four years on program book covers and T-shirts.

The cover of the 1988 Glen Echo Irish Festival program book. Or was it 1989, or maybe 1990? Thanks to my photo cropping, we may never know.

**15th Annual Washington, D.C.**

# Irish Folk Festival

**Glen Echo Park
May 26, 1991**

In 1991, we finally faced facts and did a different cover design - although it still featured the fiddle. Suzanne McMenamin was the designer. The 1991 program was also notable for containing four essays by noted folklorists in addition to the performer bios - a practice we were to continue in subsequent years.

*In 1992 we commissioned and paid a Canadian artist named Krista Howell to do a festival design for us. We weren't really pleased with the end result, so the only place it appeared was on the cover of the program book. We used something else for the T shirt.*

*For the first festival at Wolf Trap in 1993 we finally got away from using the fiddle on the program book and T shirt. Cover design was by Jon Gann. We never did find out why the accordion player had to wear white gloves.*

The 1994 program book cover art was by Patrick Gallagher, a popular crafts demonstrator and vendor at the festival for many years.

We had to produce the Irish Festival CD we did in 1994 on the cheap since we would be using it for fundraising, not selling it. I did the CD sleeve myself using Microsoft Publisher.

The 1995 program book cover was designed by Carol Hardy and featured a photograph by Bob Barrett of a hand-crafted brooch by Linda Hickman. Linda was a festival fixture as a flute player in Celtic Thunder and a jewelry maker in the Crafts area.

The cover of the 1996 program book was a painting by J.B. Vallely of Armagh, father of Cillian and Niall who both appeared several times at the Festival as members of Lunasa and Nomos respectively. I always liked J.B. Vallely's paintings of Irish trad musicians, and now have a couple of prints of his work hanging on my living room wall.

The 1997 program book cover was a collage of photos from previous Irish Festivals at Wolf Trap. The designer was Dan Kaufman.

The program book cover for the 1998 festival - the first one to have two days of programming over Labor Day Weekend at the Montgomery County Fairgrounds - featured original art by Kevin Dillon.

The 1999 program book cover design was the weakest of all of them, in my opinion. It is credited in the book to Zamore Design.

*The cover of the 24th and last Washington Irish Folk Festival, held at the Montgomery County Fairgrounds in Gaithersburg, MD, September 2-3, 2000. No credit is given in the book to the cover designer.*

## The Festival: Wolf Trap and Beyond

Despite the great success we'd had building the festival at Glen Echo, with each new year it became ever more clear that we couldn't continue it there. This was partly due to logistical concerns, the decrepit Glen Echo site having no facilities whatsoever for creating a "green room" area where performers could go when they were not on stage, or where VIPs like the Irish Ambassador could be hosted. But the biggest problem with Glen Echo was the Park Service's repressive rules that would not allow us to charge admission to the event or have food and merchandise vendors on site, even though that was a basic expectation of patrons coming from out of town to what had become a prestigious event. Fortunately, an angel arrived when Sandy Walter moved to Washington to become deputy director of the NPS National Capital Region. Sandy – who sadly died early in 2011 – was a longtime supporter of traditional arts and the then-girlfriend and future wife of Irish fiddler Seamus Connolly, who had played often at our festival. Through lots of meetings and with lots of grant proposal writing on the part of myself and others, Sandy managed to get the festival into Wolf Trap – totally against the will of the Wolf Trap staff.

Having attended many concerts and even an occasional festival at Wolf Trap over the years, I could never really understand their reluctance to embrace the Irish Festival. Although we did miss the "fading elegance" of Glen Echo, Wolf Trap proved to be an ideal venue for the festival. The massive green room area in the Filene Center was perfect for day-long performer hospitality, and for the first time we were able to run a separate-admission evening concert in the outdoor amphitheater after a full day of tent performances at six outdoor stages erected around the tree-filled Wolf Trap grounds. Sitting on my bookshelves now are VHS tapes of shows produced by WNVT-TV from footage shot at the evening concerts during the Wolf Trap years. These shows aired on public television stations in Washington and New York, which greatly helped to expand the festival's profile – and Wolf Trap's as well. We were also able to use these videos for future fundraising, just as we had started to do at Glen Echo.

So after the first Irish Festival there, it seemed that the move to Wolf Trap was an unqualified success – but a faction of the Ceili Club did not feel that way at all. One thing I had learned very early on in my exposure to things Irish was that there could never be just one organization in town promoting any aspect of Irish culture. There were always at least two, but they would invariably be able to trace themselves back to a single source. Irish emigrants or Irish Americans of enthusiasm and vision would struggle to establish a beachhead of organization and structure, but eventually – and frequently not long after the ink on the bylaws was dry – factions would form and a second competing organization would be spawned. This typically Irish behavior mirrored the behavior of the Irish nation itself, which immediately after succeeding in a centuries-long struggle to gain its independence from Britain turned on itself in a vicious Civil War. The civil war within the GWCC over the fate of the Irish Festival was not vicious, but it was indeed a war.

Despite the success of the first festival at Wolf Trap, a group of Ceili Club board members was worried that the scope and budget of the event had grown so large. They were afraid that if there ever was a bad year for the festival, the resulting failure would pull down the club's ability to produce its monthly dances and the annual Cape May Ceili Weekend that everyone loved. In fairness to them, the dance events *were* the reason the Ceili Club existed in the first place, so they had a very valid point. When it came time for the annual GWCC Board elections, there were 10 seats open for re-election according to the bylaws. The anti-festival faction resolved to put together a slate of candidates to run for the open seats, which if they won all of them would have given them the majority on the board and enabled them to eliminate or scale back the Irish Festival. Normally there was no contest for a seat on the board, in fact there often needed to be a lot of cajoling done to get someone to agree to run for an open seat. That was not the case in 1993, as the anti-Festival faction was able to put together a slate of candidates headed by Tricia McGillan running for the open President spot.

Faced with this, the pro-Festival faction needed to retaliate by coming up with its own slate, which we did – even though we were only able to find eight candidates, leaving two slots still in play. Ceili Club elections were typically very low in turnout, and there were no provisions for mail-in ballots or any other such thing. There was no way to know which way the vote would ultimately go. But fortunately there was a provision in the Ceili Club bylaws that allowed someone to join the club on the day of an election and cast a vote, and that proved to be the Irish Festival's salvation. When it was all over, Bob Hickey – a member of the anti-Festival slate – submitted an article for the GWCC Newsletter describing the goings-on. I don't believe it was ever printed in the newsletter, though, so I'll print it here, two decades too late. There's not a word in it that's not the truth.

*ELECTION HIGH-JINKS by Bob Hickey*

*For those of you who missed the Dec. 4th club elections, you missed quite a show. Just before the elections were to begin, almost miraculously, 31 new members showed up, joined the club, voted and help* [sic] *sweep Mr. Denney and the entire Celtic Outreach slate into office. Diana and Ron Jensen were also elected to the Board of Directors as Celtic Outreach only had 8 candidates for the 10 position board. Some members have suggested that the McMillan* [sic] *slate was out-foxed by the opposition. That is not true. We were expecting some Tammany-Hall tactics.*

*Several days before the election I received a telephone call from a local musician who advised me that he had received a telephone call from Mike Denney. He said that Mike asked him to come to the elections, join the club and vote for his slate. He offered to pay the musician's dues in return for his vote.*

*So the McMillan* [sic] *slate knew it was coming and we discussed retaliation in-kind. I know many local musicians who would have joined, and voted with a vengeance. We decided however (unanimously) that it would be unethical to bring in a bunch of "ringers" to win the election. For some, "ethical" is a test that guides their conduct; for others, "winning is everything", "ethical" is only a word in the dictionary.*

*This vote, we thought, was to be a referendum on what the club wanted; Fiscal Responsibility or Festival Roulette (as I like to call it).*

*The election produced some interesting new members, prominent among them was the well known Washington publican: Hugh Kelly, owner of the Irish Times Tavern. You don't have to worry which way he voted when you remember all of the lavish pre-festival parties held in his pub. (Hugh promised me he would vote for me next year.) Seeing John Kerr's mother and father join the club and vote reinforced for me the importance of "family values." In hindsight, we should have had Darcy and Maddie Byrnes join the club and vote for their mom and dad!*

*Alas, it's over and we will sit on the sidelines in '94 nursing our disappointment but resolved to continue to support the Ceilis and Concerts, the wonderful weekend at Cape May (thank you Ron and Diana) and the 94 festival. Now that Mr. Denney has gotten rid of the malecontents* [sic] *and obstructionists, the 94 festival is bound to be bigger and better. Good luck and remember what Shakespeare says "everything comes around."*

(For the record, my parents paid their own membership fee. I didn't pay it for them. And when their membership came up for renewal the next year, they renewed. And they continued to renew year after year even though they never went to any activities other than the festival. Indeed, I was surprised to learn a year or two after I had let my own GWCC membership lapse that they were still renewing theirs. I should mention that to Bob sometime.)

Of the fifteen Washington Irish Festivals I was involved in, the 1994 event was by far the most memorable, for two reasons. First, it featured the grand comeback to the Irish button accordion of Joe Derrane. Joe had been a child prodigy on the D/C# box in Boston in the 1940s, and recorded a seminal series of 78s when he was but a teenager. These recordings made their way to Ireland, where Joe eventually became known as an iconic player by such luminaries as Frankie Gavin of DeDannan. But since Joe had left the world of Irish trad music in the 1950s to play the more lucrative show band music then in demand in Boston's dance halls, most everyone who knew of his button accordion playing thought him to be long dead. But in late 1993 the Irish music writer Earle Hitchner discovered Joe living in retirement in Boston, and challenged him to play the button box again with the carrot of a guaranteed gig at the Wolf Trap festival if he did. Joe's appearance at the 1994 Festival was an unqualified success, and represented the beginning of a second recording and performing career for him that is still going strong. In the annals of Irish music history, Joe Derrane and the Wolf Trap Irish Festival are forever linked.

The second memory of that year's festival is an incredibly sad one. Frankie Kennedy of Altan, the great Belfast flute player, had been battling cancer for some two years when the band arrived at Wolf Trap that weekend. He was in remission, but still was not seen much at any Festival parties or backstage events over the weekend as he was resting at the hotel. But for the band's stage sets he was in top form, playing as well as he ever had, driving the stage banter with his dry Belfast wit, and enjoying himself immensely. The band returned to Ireland, and a scant four months later he was dead, still in his prime at age 39. So one day had seen both the grand re-emergence of a legend of Irish music and the tragic and premature end to the life of another. No other festival packed so much raw emotion as this one did.

But there were always moments of levity too. It was either the 1993 or 1994 festival when I was driving the shuttle van back to the Phoenix Park Hotel on Capitol Hill, which is where we housed the festival performers in the Glen Echo and Wolf Trap years. The members of

Altan were in the van as I drove down the Dulles Airport road toward I-66, and a stretch limo passed us on the left. Either Frankie Kennedy or Ciaran Tourish happened to look down into the limo as it passed and yelled out *Hey, there's a couple in there doing it!* They immediately implored me to catch up to the limo again, but the limo driver must have realized that they'd been spotted because no matter how hard I tried to maneuver through traffic to pull up next to them, I never could.

We always had made recordings off the sound board at each stage during the festival, but never really did anything with them other than pass bootleg copies around to the festival in-crowd. But after the 1994 event, we teamed up with Jeff Place of Smithsonian Folkways to produce a CD of highlights that we then offered in subsequent years as a give-away to people donating to the festival. Several of us on the Entertainment Committee got together for listening and discussion sessions over the better part of a year, and then went down to Jeff's Smithsonian studio for the final mix off the master tapes. I still have a copy of this CD, and it is definitely something I need to find a place for out on the Internet so more people can hear this great music – copyrights be damned!

By 1995 the Festival was firmly entrenched at Wolf Trap – or so we thought. Things would change in a few years. But at least for a while, Memorial Day weekends settled into a nice rhythm for me. Following several months of hard work, writing most of the program book content and chairing the Entertainment Committee, Friday night and Saturday afternoon would find me driving a van out to either Dulles or National Airport to pick up the performers as their flights came in, and ferrying them back to the Phoenix Park Hotel, which was party central for the weekend. In those innocent pre-9/11 days, when picking up passengers at an airport you could walk clear through to the gate and meet them right as they walked off the plane. One of those times as I stood at a gate waiting for a performer's flight to taxi in, I looked up – and leaning on a column directly across from me was former Surgeon General C. Everett Koop, waiting on someone himself. I managed to refrain from asking him what the deal was with the chin-strap beard.

In picking up performers at the airport, I never wanted to be the guy standing there with a poster board with their name printed on it. So I spent a lot of time running back and forth between the short-term parking garage and the gates so I wouldn't be late and miss connecting with them. I was usually successful, although there was the one time I had to chase down dancer Liam Harney who decided to rollerblade through the long concourse to the baggage claim when I wasn't there at the gate to greet him right when he came off the plane. I was acutely aware that I would be these artists' first impression of the DC area, but there were a few times I had some help from nice weather. I remember when Fiona Ritchie of the radio show *Thistle and Shamrock,* who was our evening concert MC during the Wolf Trap years, got off the plane for the third straight year on a beautiful, sunny, crisp early summer day, so uncommon in Washington. *Did it ever rain when the Festival was at Glen Echo?* she asked. I think it was the next day that we had our first rainstorm at a Wolf Trap festival, which set us on the way to the yearly deluges that ultimately drowned the entire event.

On Saturday night, it was time to ferry whatever musicians were booked to play the Festival Ceili out to the Spanish Ballroom and back. (Our last hold on Glen Echo, as there was nowhere at Wolf Trap to hold a proper ceili.) In 1995, the ceili band was a group called Moving Cloud, which included a flute player called Kevin Crawford –

my first meeting with that man of the outsize personality who I've had the pleasure of seeing somewhere pretty much every year since. I've even been known to take flute classes with him solely for the comedy, the tunes just being the icing on the cake.

Sunday mornings of festival weekends it was time to make several van runs back and forth from the Phoenix Park Hotel to Wolf Trap to get the performers out there, a process that would be repeated in reverse after the evening concert. It was one of the Wolf Trap years when I had my first experience of the annual Memorial Day Vietnam veterans' event called Rolling Thunder. Heading back to DC in the van on an otherwise deserted I-395, just before the 14th Street Bridge I was suddenly surrounded by motorcycles, like a swarm of hornets whose nest just got disturbed. Back then, the veterans on motorcycles would be concentrated in certain areas near the monuments and Arlington Cemetery. Now, though, on Memorial Day Weekend if you live anywhere within 25 miles of DC, you can't open your window without hearing the buzz of motorcycles.

Sunday night after the festival was over always featured an all-night party in the penthouse suite of the Phoenix Park. I think those of us on the Entertainment Committee thought of the party as a good excuse to have a festival, rather than the other way around. We always felt that the main thing that made performers think so highly of our festival was that we treated them right. We were never able to pay them the big bucks they might command at other festivals or venues, but we compensated for that by always treating them with the utmost respect and by making their comfort and happiness our number one priority. The Sunday night party was a big part of that. It gave the many different groups of musicians and dancers on the program, who otherwise spend their touring lives passing like ships in the night, a chance to sit down, relax, enjoy each other's company, and make new connections. In theory the whole festival weekend provided that opportunity, but musicians and dancers are nocturnal people and the daylight hours were spent either sleeping or performing. So the Festival Party came at just the right time, with their work for the weekend over and the whole night ahead of them before they had to travel home. We placed no expectations on any of the performers for the party. They could play music if they wanted to, or they could just hang out to eat, drink and talk. Since even the hotel's biggest space was still a fairly small room, we had to keep the guest list limited, which did engender some resentment among festival attendees and volunteers who weren't allowed in. Having what seemed to be an exclusive party was probably bad for our festival brand, but it paid dividends with the performers who could relax completely without having to worry about being "on." Sometimes that relaxation spilled out of the penthouse party suite and into the rest of the hotel, and in at least one memorable case outside of the hotel entirely when there was (step)dancing in the street in the wee hours. But that was never an issue, because we always conveniently made sure that there was no one staying in the Phoenix Park that weekend who was not affiliated with the festival.

Alas, unlike the other after-parties I got to attend in those days I was never fully able to enter into the spirit of the Festival Party. I was not "on the clock" while the parties were going on, but I had to be ready to drive people to the airport bright and early in the morning. Since the Festival always booked their flights, and since we had to keep them as cheap as possible, we frequently had someone on the first flight out of National Airport, which left before dawn. At least it felt like that, anyway. Maybe it's because I was never fully able to get into the party spirit like everyone else that I can still recall all these details of all those Festival weekends. I hope that none of the stuff I have been able to recall proves incriminating for anyone!

The 1995 Festival was also notable for being (as far as I can tell from the program books, anyway) the first appearance of Patrick and Sean McComiskey and Matt Mulqueen, who played on the Next Generation stage along with Brendan Callahan, Patrick Mangan and Matt and Aaron Olwell. Kids back then, now fully grown friends of mine (Facebook and real life too), several of them with kids of their own. God I feel old.

1997 was the 20th staging of the Washington Irish Festival, and after ten years of GWCC sponsorship it also represented the realization that – despite what we had all thought, hoped and attempted – there was no way the festival could survive as an all-volunteer event. There was simply too much involved to entrust the production of an event that had become known both in Ireland and America as one of the finest of its kind to a group of organizers who were stealing time from their day jobs and real lives. Fortunately a professional traditional arts organization was at hand who were willing to take over responsibility for the Festival – the National Council for the Traditional Arts, based in Silver Spring, for many years the producers of the National Folk Festival and many other events. Chris Williams of NCTA took the position of Associate Director to Mike Denney's Director in this transitional year, and by 1998 official GWCC involvement in the Irish Festival was strictly a memory – although many of us continued to help the NCTA as volunteers.

The good news for me was that this move greatly lessened the amount of work I had to do for the festival, and correspondingly gave me more time to enjoy it in what were unfortunately to become the golden years of its 24-year lifetime. I no longer had to write the extensive program notes, but stayed as part of the Program Committee with two major duties each year – driving performers back and forth as I had done already for several years, and working with Jeff Place of the Smithsonian on the audio archiving of the festival performances. The big benefit of that was that I was one of the few people who got to hear every single note played at the event – a feat which couldn't be accomplished physically since we had up to six stages running simultaneously. But every year before I handed the tapes over to NCTA I had to give them a listen – for "quality control" purposes, of course – and more than a few of them ended up being copied over to cassette for my personal collection. I still have these tapes laying around the house somewhere. More stuff that I really need to find the technology and time to digitize.

Although we didn't know it at the time, the 1997 Festival would be the last one at Wolf Trap, and the last one on Memorial Day weekend. The biggest memory for me of this festival was the visit of the legendary Tulla Ceili Band of Co. Clare, celebrating the release of their 50th anniversary recording. The band was still headed up by the esteemed and influential fiddler P. Joe Hayes, although its biggest star was his son Martin, who was then and still is now one of the most original and iconic musicians to ever come out of Ireland. I had met up with the band the previous November when they started their grand year-long celebration of their 50th anniversary at the Green Linnet Irish Music Party in the Catskills. (Someone should write a book about those weekends. Green Linnet Records never really knew how to make money – much less pay royalties – but boy did they know how to throw a party.) At the Green Linnet weekend I had the Tulla Band's box player Sean Donnelly as my roommate, and I think that whole weekend he never changed out of the suit he was wearing, even to sleep. And sleeping was about the only time he spent in the room, too. On Saturday night he was out playing all night, went to Mass on Sunday morning and then came back to bed, still in the suit.

For the Wolf Trap Festival weekend I basically served as the band's chauffeur. Normally I would have been driving a nine passenger van – still somewhat manageable for a small-car driver like myself – but the size of the Tulla Band and all their equipment forced us to rent a 15 passenger van, a true land yacht. It wasn't really an issue picking them up at the airport in that behemoth, or taking them out to Glen Echo on Saturday night for the ceili or to Wolf Trap on Sunday for the festival. Wide open spaces there. But all weekend long I was sweating what was to come on Monday night. It was a festival tradition to take whatever straggler performers were still around on Monday night out to Nanny O'Brien's for the session. The Tulla was still going to be in town, and they would need to get to Nanny's and back to the hotel. Normally, parking around Nanny's is a real pain. Most Mondays when I'd go to the session I would end up parking several blocks away, and even then it was rare to find even the smallest of parking spaces to put my little VW in. I had visions of driving the big van up to the curb in front of Nanny's, unloading all of them and their instruments, and then driving around for four hours until last call because I wouldn't be able to park the van and go into the session myself. But lo and behold, just as we rolled up Connecticut Avenue there appeared two adjacent empty parking spaces right in front of the Nanny's door! I quickly steered the van in, we all got out and went in for one of the most memorable sessions in Nanny's history. A true moment of festival sunshine – and as it turned out, possibly the last one, as will be seen from the accounts of subsequent years.

As I mentioned when I wrote of the Festival moving from Glen Echo to Wolf Trap, Wolf Trap never really wanted us there. And with our National Park Service connection Sandy Walter having moved up to Boston to be with Seamus Connolly a few years before, by 1998 Wolf Trap started twisting the screws to get rid of us. The 1997 Festival had been hit by a bit of rain (a harbinger of things to come) and the crowd walking around to the outside tents had mussed up Wolf Trap's sacred grounds. (Which actually were nothing but National Park space that never got used for anything else during the year that would benefit the taxpaying public, but let's not go there now...) Wolf Trap proposed a massive cutback in the scope of the event, which was a non-starter from the moment they brought it up. The NCTA folks scrambled and came up with an alternative site, the Montgomery County Fairgrounds in Gaithersburg. But unlike the move from Glen Echo to Wolf Trap, this turned out to be more than a mere change in venue. The Fairgrounds were already booked in perpetuity on Memorial Day weekend, so the Festival had to be moved to Labor Day weekend. That carried a couple of bright spots with it, since for the first time the event could be expanded to two full days, and also there were several hotels within sight of the Fairgrounds that could be used to house performers and visitors. No more shuttling back and forth from the Phoenix Park Hotel on Capitol Hill. The Festival could now become a self-contained weekend-long destination event.

But there turned out to be a few downsides to a Labor Day Festival at the Fairgrounds. The massive Montgomery County Fair ended right before the Festival, but its animal odors remained. The non-Irish Holiday Inn and Hilton staff were not as understanding of the Irish notion of *craic* as the Irish-immigrant Phoenix Park staff had been. None of the Fairgrounds Festival parties ended up matching the legendary days of the Phoenix Park. And the biggest change of moving to Labor Day proved to be one of climate. While we had experienced our fair share of thunderstorms disrupting the Memorial Day weekend, there was not the potential for days and days of monsoon conditions as there is on Labor Day, it being smack in the middle of hurricane season. It was this change of climate that ultimately ended up doing the Festival in.

But all that was yet to come. The 1998 Festival at the Fairgrounds was, as I recall, an unqualified success. And for me the biggest memory of that year is that we were able to bring the great Dublin singer Frank Harte (who had become a good friend of mine thanks to many meetings over the years at Augusta Irish Week) over for the Festival. Frank's presence, along with that of Brendan Begley of the band Beginish, ended up turning the Monday night session after the Festival into perhaps the greatest session night ever at Nanny O'Brien's, as I mentioned earlier in this book.

Theoretically, making the Festival a two-day event was supposed to decrease its vulnerability to weather calamities. Indeed, I seem to recall that even the 1998 Festival, success that it was, saw some rain over the course of the weekend – but the periods of sunshine over the rest of Saturday and Sunday were more than enough to make up for it. But the theory was put to the test and proved to be just so much bunk over Labor Day weekend 1999, when the remnants of Hurricane Dennis turned the Montgomery County Fairgrounds into a sea of mud.

Barnyard-smelly mud, to be exact. But the first rule of showbiz is that the show must go on, and so the Festival did, with a few changes on account of the weather. The evening concert sets had to be moved from the outdoor Maple Avenue Stage to the covered Cattle Barn, which was much drier – although also more smelly. But whatever malodorous smells were in the air that weekend, none came from the performances, which were all top-notch. Kevin Crawford was ubiquitous, appearing in two sets each day with both Lunasa and Moving Cloud. Yet on both Saturday and Sunday mornings when I stumbled groggily into the hotel lobby after a late night before, the first person I encountered was a chipper Kevin – already back from his daily run! Where he finds the energy, I'll never know.

The 1999 Festival featured perhaps the largest bunch of bands and musicians "direct from Ireland" (as they say) that the Washington Irish Festival had ever assembled. In addition to the previously-mentioned Lunasa and Moving Cloud, Beginish (Brendan Begley, Paul McGrattan, Paul O'Shaughnessy and Noel O'Grady), Calico (Tola Custy, Donncha, Diarmuid and Deirdre Moynihan and Pat Marsh) and Danu (featuring Baltimore's own Jesse Smith) also graced the stages of the Festival. But the home front was well represented, too, including an early appearance of the Pride of New York (Billy McComiskey, Brian Conway, Joanie Madden and Brendan Dolan) who went on to release a landmark recording a full decade later.

By Y2K the Festival's unofficial motto had become "There's no fecking way it can rain as much this year as it did last year!" Yet somehow it still did, and the rains of Labor Day 2000 were enough to wash the Washington Irish Festival away for good – although we didn't know it at the time. The 24th and last Irish Festival did at least go out with a bang. In addition to perennial favorites like Lunasa, Dervish, Danu, Cherish the Ladies and Liz Carroll, the 2000 Festival featured acts not often seen in Washington, like the Kathryn Tickell Band and Paddy Glackin with Robbie Hannan. As I recall, we were able to bask in the high of these great performances until around November, when word started going around that the future of the event was in jeopardy. The NCTA staff did not dither about it, but pulled the plug fairly quickly.

NCTA had been running the Festival for four years at that point, and if anything they had upped the ante over the already high standards set by GWCC. We former festival organizers who were no longer privy to the inner financial workings of the event could do nothing but marvel at its continued ability to attract so many of the finest musicians in Ireland and America. NCTA truly spared no expense, and after four years of declining gate receipts due to bad weather it was not a big surprise that they were forced to pull the plug on the event. At first, it was going to be "let's take a year off," but we all know how that goes. Each successive year off from such a massive undertaking makes it that much harder to ever get it started up again.

In the end, Bob Hickey's Shakespeare quote from 1993 had come true – for him, at least. "Everything comes around." After leaving the Irish Festival, Bob became the founding chairman of a new branch of Comhaltas Ceoltoiri Eireann (the Irish musicians' organization) in Washington, and for many years his CCE chapter has run an annual festival that in its good years matches the small, mainly local Glen Echo Irish Festivals of 1985 and 1986, when the GWCC took over and this saga began. That's a good thing. But even though it's over a decade now since it ended, if I ever happen to mention the Irish

Festivals of Glen Echo and Wolf Trap to someone, invariably they ask me *Do you think it will ever come back?*

My answer has to be no. The festival did grow organically out of basically nothing over the 15 years I was involved with it, so I suppose the same thing could happen again, say with the CCE Festival. But it would require two things that I don't think will come together again. The first would be a leader with the vision, drive, persistence and thick skin of Mike Denney, who truly had the controlling hand over the festival through practically its entire 15 year run of glory. Even after it was handed over to NCTA and he was no longer the director, he still had a big say in what went on. But one man could never have pulled off what the festival did over the years without also having a large and dedicated group of people working with him. Until the festival was transferred to NCTA, the only festival workers who were paid anything at all were the performers and sound technicians on the day of the event. Everyone else was a volunteer, and I was far from alone in being someone who devoted several hundred hours of my own time – and, the statute of limitations having been reached, many hours of my employer's time as well – to working on the festival. There were folks who, like me, were involved for the whole 15 year run, and there were folks who were around at the beginning but dropped out before the end, or folks who came along in the Wolf Trap days and stuck it out until the very end. The only way I can possibly remember them all is to look back at the Festival Committee lists in the yearly program books, where I find these names: Jesse Winch and his wife Francesca Lee, Marsha Maguire, Mike and Kathy Kevany, Jim Owens and his late wife Micki Loughlin and current wife Marilyn Moore, Mike Tivnan, Steve Lourie, Don Schuirmann, Bob Hickey and his wife Kate Kane, Diana and Ron Jensen, Rob and his late wife Stephanie Byrnes,

Terry Winch and his wife Susan Campbell, Judy Walsh, the late Mary LaMarca, Jim Beamer, Joan O'Connell, Michael and Marleen Denney, Suzanne McMenamin, Dave Harmen, Andrea Blackburn, Chris O'Brien, the late Bill Whitman, Dwain Winters and his wife Beth Curren, Alicia Kraft, Barry Stohlman, Clare Stohlman Langley, Linda Mason, Kathy O'Rourke, Mary Boeckman, Jim Burns, Maureen Tighe, Neil Beskin and his wife Trudie Cushing, Misa Acox, Tricia McGillan, Linda Fotis, Carol Ropiak, Cathi Smith O'Neill, John Duffy, Carly Gewirz, Melissa McDowell, Trish Callahan, Sue Casey, Jeff Place, Helen Anderson, Paul and Edie O'Donnell, Alan Bubna, Linda Jeffers, Jane Twomey, John Faulkner, Dick DeFreyre and his wife Dixie Baker, Tim Meagher, Ginny Kelly, Cecilia Farley, Dan Sullivan, Mike Mangan, Bill DeGraff and Katie King.

Beyond these names, there were literally hundreds of others who volunteered their time – without having to suffer through the never-ending festival committee meetings, but also without the glory of having their name listed in the program book – to keep the festival going and growing for 15 years. Every one of their individual contributions could almost be considered essential, because as I hope you can see from this narrative the festival was basically hanging by a thread for the entirety of its run. I really can't imagine another group of people coming together and being able to pull off a similar task again. I'm just glad that all of us were able to do it the one time, for fifteen memorable years.

## The Ceili

I think it was Frank Zappa who said that writing about music is like dancing about architecture. If so, it's pretty clear he never encountered any Irish traditional musicians or dancers. Other than for jotting down the words to a song or the notes to a tune so you don't forget them, writing is of no real use to the traditional musician. Indeed, I've met many fine trad musicians who don't read music at all, and even one (the late Mike Rafferty) who didn't even know the names of the notes he was playing! In contrast, one of the first things I learned when I started doing ceili and set dancing is that Irish dancing is *all* about architecture. Three kinds of architecture, to be specific: the shoe store, the laundry room and – most of all – the floor.

I was barely into my first set dancing class with Mike Denney when I realized that just any old shoe wouldn't do. To do the fancy toe and heel taps with the strategically-placed weight shifts that together define the rhythm of the polka, reel, jig or hornpipe figures, you need a shoe with a pretty hard sole. Doesn't have to be as hard as the stepdancer's shoe that in the old days was fortified with nails in the sole and now is made of fiberglass or other such high-tech material, but it has to be hard enough to make some noise on the floor. But it can't be done with sheer mass, like a combat boot, because aside from the rhythm the next most noticeable aspect of Irish dancing is how the best dancers seem almost to hover over the floor and reach down to touch it, rather than being anchored to the floor and leaping up off it. There's an old phrase that describes the dancing. *Dance like a wave of the sea.* You really have no hope of doing that if you're wearing an anchor on both of your feet. So once I got into dancing, it was off to the shoe store I went, to buy leather-soled shoes that were useless anywhere but on the dance floor or at the stodgiest of weddings. And there are two things about those shoes. They're hard to find, and they don't come cheap. Which is why, over the course of my dancing career, my architectural tour did not stop at the shoe store. I also learned about the shoe repair shop, where I could get new leather soles put on my expensive, hard-to-find shoes every year or so. I was never quite on a first-name basis with my cobbler, but I'm pretty sure it wasn't Dick Darby. He did a good job, though, and saved me a good few bucks over what buying new shoes every six months would have cost.

Above the ankle, though, I found that the specifics of ceili attire were not all that critical. It certainly wouldn't have been cool for a guy to wear a skirt or even a dress to a ceili, like I saw some guys doing at the contradances that went on in the same Glen Echo ballroom where Mike Denney had his dance classes. And whenever a guy showed up trying to look "authentic" by wearing a kilt, he got looked at askance and never got a good dance partner. But other than that, pretty much all you needed in your ceili wardrobe was a shirt and pants. Check that – you needed *multiple* shirts. At least one per hour of the ceili, at a minimum. That old axiom that says "horses sweat, men perspire and women glow" is true. And while a glowing woman has no qualms about riding a sweating horse, she's going to think twice before accepting an invitation to dance when it comes from a man soaked with perspiration. Except for the dead of winter, I found I could barely make it through the four or five or six figures of one set without soaking completely through my shirt. My only hope of being able to dance for an entire evening was to start bringing half my wardrobe to each and every ceili. I was never so happy to be living in a place where

I had my own washing machine and dryer and didn't have to go to the basement to feed quarters into the communal laundry facilities. I also tended to buy my dancing shirts in bulk. Since this was before the days of my Costco membership, I was shopping by mail from the likes of L.L. Bean and Lands' End. At one time I had about five different vertically-striped button-down-collar shirts in assorted colors that I wore at ceilis. Then one day Barry Stohlman said to me *Don't you ever wear anything besides striped shirts?* and I was forced to jettison my entire dance wardrobe and start all over again.

In those days I used to place a little tick mark on my desk calendar for any day that I went to a dance or dance class. In one year in the late 1980s, I think I had about 200 tick marks on my calendar, which meant that I was out dancing at least every other day. Such public visibility made it inevitable that I'd be asked to join the board of the Greater Washington Ceili Club, the group that produced most of the dances and classes I attended. I think it was Joan O'Connell or Suzanne McMenamin who convinced me by saying *It's easy. We just sit around Ron and Diana's living room and talk about the ceili* – Diana Jensen being the founding president of the GWCC and the co-owner of that living room with her husband Ron. Of course what Joan or Suzanne *didn't* tell me was that I'd gain 15 pounds from all the cakes and snack foods that showed up on Ron and Diana's coffee table while we were sitting around talking about the ceili. I joined the board right around the time that Entenmann's and Snackwell's fat-free cakes became all the rage. People give fat a bad rap, but they fail to realize that it does a lot of things that are actually *good* for you. It magnifies and carries flavors onto the taste buds, and it fills you up, satiating you so that eventually you'll stop eating whatever it is you're enjoying. Take all the fat out of a cake, and there's nothing left to tell you that you've had enough. I was feeling real good about myself towards the end of one board meeting since I'd only eaten half of one of the fat-free coffee cakes that graced the table when the meeting started. Then I looked at the nutrition information on the side of the box. Ten servings per box. 200 calories per serving. I had five servings. That's *1000 calories*. But hey….zero grams fat. No wonder I was gaining weight, despite all the dancing and sweating through of shirts I was doing.

When we weren't chowing down or talking about the ceili, it soon became clear that the GWCC Board's main, perhaps only *raison d'etre* was to find and rent floor space. (Again with the architecture.) And not just any floor space. It needed to be hard, but not *too* hard. Needed to have some spring to it. Wood, not concrete – and definitely not carpeted. Also, there needed to be enough of it to hold a hundred or so dancers in square sets of eight, with room along the side for people to sit and for all the male dancers to stash their many changes of clothes. And, oh, one other thing. It had to be available cheap. We only charged those hundred or so dancers eight bucks to get in, so out of the hoped-for 800 bucks we had to pay for both the hall and the band.

It turned out that the first GWCC Ceili I ever went to happened to be at the perfect venue. I have no idea how the GWCC got there, but I just assumed that Irish ceilis were always held at places like the Kennedy-Warren Ballroom. How naïve I was! Located just a few doors down Connecticut Avenue (albeit across the Klingle Valley Bridge) from my future session pub, Nanny O'Brien's – which was still in its earlier incarnation as Gallagher's at the time – the Kennedy-Warren Apartments are an Art Deco masterpiece, perhaps the finest such building in Washington. Buried deep within that building is a magnificent ballroom. Hardwood floor, massive stage, ringed by a mezzanine level where tables could be set up for non-dancers to have a clear view of all the goings-on on the stage or the dance floor. Ornate chandeliers and classic Art Deco decor and trim throughout. I can only imagine the marvelous nights of big band and jazz music and dancing that had taken place there since the building was constructed in the early 1930s, or the famous performers who undoubtedly appeared there over the years. Somehow, some way, by the late 1980s this marvelous space had become the home of the GWCC's monthly ceili, held on the fourth Sunday in the late afternoon/early evening, since that's when no one else wanted to rent the space and we could get it cheap. A brief dance lesson beforehand, pot luck supper during the first break, and music by the Celtic Thunder Ceili Band were staples of the GWCC Ceili experience. I had seen the notice in the monthly GWCC newsletter for almost a year, after I saw Irish ceili dancing for the first time at the Augusta Irish Week, then found a flyer on the table at one of the Friday night contradances I was frequenting at the time, and impulsively decided to join. Finally I mustered the nerve to actually go to a ceili, found my way to the Kennedy-Warren, and walked to the table to pay my way in. Stephanie Byrnes, who was working the door, gave me a strange look when I told her I qualified for the member rate. At that time the GWCC was so small that everyone knew everybody, and somehow my disembodied name on the member list had escaped notice. But soon enough it was all sorted out, and I was in.

Although in reality the process probably took about a year, it seemed as if immediately after I obtained entrance to that first GWCC Ceili I found myself traveling a circuit of the local ceilis along with a group of rabid dancers including Sue Casey, Barry and Clare Stohlman, George Kuhn, Suzanne McMenamin, Alicia Kraft, Joan O'Connell and several others. As I've noted elsewhere, one of the prime defining characteristics of an Irish scene in any local area is the presence of more than one group promoting the same aspect of Irishness, be it dancing or music or sports or whatever. Internal dissension always arises in the first group to emerge on the scene, and rather than work things out the dissenters always split off and form another group doing the very same thing as the first group. The more groups that survive this process, the healthier the scene. The Irish social dancing scene was so healthy when my friends and I embarked on our ceili tour that there were three monthly ceilis in the DC area, each sponsored by a different organization. They all descended from one source, but the intricacies of who-begat-whom were never clear to me. (Just like the intricacies of when to use who and when to use whom, for that matter.) Depending on who you talked to, either Peggy O'Neill ADCRG (whose disciples spawned what became the Vienna ceili) or Harry and Margaret Schrecengost (who founded and ran the Blackthorn Stick) were the source well for ceili dancing in the Washington area. But one thing was certain. The Greater Washington Ceili Club was the new kid on the block. Its founders came from the other groups, and the dissension that caused them to form a new group was not the usual personality conflicts (although to be sure there were a few of those in play) but rather the desire to dance the country sets that were then enjoying a revival in Ireland. Those dances were not then to be found at any ceilis in the area, where the so-called "ceili dances" ruled the floor.

The strict definition of what is a "ceili dance" is any dance that appears in the book *Ár Rincí Fóirne* put out by the Irish Dance Commission. The older ceili groups in DC had raised those officially-sanctioned dances like the Sweets of May, the High Cauld Cap, the

Sixteen Hand Reel and the Three Tunes to the status of high art. Their monthly ceilis had more of the aspects of ceremony than the feel of a social occasion. The best of their dancers were invited to join their performing groups, don a special costume featuring a multi-colored fabric belt or some such accessory, and spend the entire St. Patrick's Day season touring and dancing at old folks' homes. Their sense of ceremony kind of reminded me of the Knights of Columbus, who with their big swoopy furry hats and swords would march down the aisle at Christmas and Easter mass in my youth. Those KofC guys knew how to party (or so said my parents, who were in on *all* the church gossip) and they also knew how to put on a show. But they always kept the party and the show separate, just like the hard core ceili dancers did. Those ceili dances were serious business. Like a stepdancer, the ceili dancer's arms and upper body didn't come into play at all, except to perform hand claps, fist thrusts and such that were tightly choreographed into particular dances. It wasn't until they got off the dance floor that ceili dancers really got down. The set dances that the GWCC made its mission to promote were different. In set dancing, the dance and the party were one and the same. The upper body was an equal part of the dancer's tool set. A *Whoop!* or a *Hup!* from one of the dancers was appropriate at any time, not just when specified by some commission in Dublin in 1930. These are the things that attracted me to set dancing and got me hooked.

The three competing groups that ran monthly ceilis in DC were all healthy, but not healthy enough to risk scheduling their dances in direct competition with each other. And although each faction in the set-dancing-versus-ceili-dancing war had enough adherents to keep a monthly dance interesting, neither had enough support to keep either an all-set-dancing or all-ceili-dancing event viable. So my dancing friends and I had the opportunity to attend a different ceili on three of the four weekends of any given month. Throw in the monthly Baltimore Ceili, and there was a dance to go to every single weekend from September through May. The Baltimore Ceili was the exception that proves the rule to my theory of how you can never have just one organization doing something Irish in a given area. While there were smaller groups of Baltimore dancers who would occasionally get together to dance in a pub or at a house party, there was only one giant ceili in town. The Baltimore Irish scene goes a lot further back than Washington's, so maybe at one time there was a split and later a merge back together. Whatever the process was, though, it was clearly fueled by beer – which flowed more freely at the Baltimore Ceili than at any other ceili I've ever seen.

Each of the four ceilis had its own personality and its own area of emphasis. The GWCC Ceili was heaviest on set dances, although the easier "group" ceili dances like the Siege of Ennis, Walls of Limerick and the like had to be included as a way of incorporating beginners and other newcomers into the dancing. Like all the ceilis back then, the GWCC had a regular band, in this case the Celtic Thunder Ceili Band, which basically was the popular and well-established band Celtic Thunder without their singer Laura Murphy – although she would sometimes show up too to sing a song during the break. The band's other singer, Dominick Murray, played guitar as well, so he was always there to sing the old-time waltzes, which were always danced to an up-tempo 3/4 song invoking the all-important themes of life such as the blessings of a mother's love, with the proper dollop of Irish guilt always thrown into the mix. The set dancing that the GWCC was championing placed greater demands on the musicians than ceili dancing did, requiring the more exotic polkas and slides for the Kerry sets in addition to the standard jigs, reels and hornpipes, and Celtic Thunder was up to the task. Their accordion player Terry Winch is a great composer of tunes in addition to being a poet and songwriter, and many of the tunes he wrote in that era were polkas and slides that the band featured every month at the Kennedy-Warren Ballroom. Terry's brother Jesse played the full trap drum set behind the band, something that was a revelation to me since I always had thought Irish music was the domain of the bodhran and the drum set was for rock music. But in Ireland, in the days before sound amplification, the ceili band of many instruments actually evolved as a way of generating enough volume to fill a big dance hall, and the drum set was central to their sound. Although in the modern era many dances take place even in Ireland without a drummer in the band, the traditional ceili band always has one in the mix. As I would come to learn in future years, as ceili drummers go you won't find a better one than Jesse Winch. And his presence in the ceili band version of Celtic Thunder was often a lifesaver for those of us on the dance floor. The Kennedy-Warren's ballroom was magnificent, but in order to get the best out of its acoustic space a good sound system was required – the likes of which could not be handled by the meager budgets of either GWCC or Celtic Thunder. Before each dance they would laboriously set up their microphones and speakers, but once the dancing started all that could reliably be heard out on the floor was the beat of the drums. That was enough for most of the dancers, but there were always a few of us who would train our ears to pick up the tunes and dance to them rather than the drums. But then things would sometimes get dicey if the band's monitors were on the fritz and the different players couldn't hear each other well enough to stay on the same beat. I recall one time when Marleen Denney, a tune-head like myself, was in the same set as me for a dance. She turned to me between figures and asked *Which musician are* you *dancing to?* Such were the perils of dancing at the GWCC Ceili, but the *craic* made it all worthwhile.

The ceili out in Vienna and the one in Baltimore actually had a lot in common. Both of them were in church halls; in Baltimore it was St. Pius X, which Mike Denney always said like it was Malcolm X instead of Pius the Tenth. The Baltimore Ceili was a lot bigger and much more raucous, maybe because as I said it was the only one in Baltimore. But more likely it was because they had beer there, and I don't recall any of that in Vienna except possibly the cooler behind the stage for the band. The band was another big similarity between the two, because Bill Whitman played at both dances. Bill was primarily a singer and a mainstay on the pub circuit, and I can't recall exactly which instrument he played in the ceili bands; probably it was guitar. But that doesn't matter, because along with whatever instrument he toted into the ceili, he brought a bag full of noisemaking tools – slide whistles, kazoos, whoopee cushions and the like. These he employed as soon as the Sweets of May was called. The Sweets of May is one of those dances that is always danced to a signature tune. And like most such signature tunes, the tune is both execrable and insidious. No matter what other great music you hear over the course of an evening, if you hear the Sweets of May it's going to be your earworm when you wake up the next day. No amount of alcohol can stop it, either. I've tried. In the Sweets of May, every time the second part rolls around, there's a bit that goes *diddly-dum* and the dancers respond with a *clap-clap*. If Bill Whitman was in the ceili band, each time the *clap-clap* rolled around you'd hear a different silly or obnoxious sound in time with the clap. That served to place the coda on that stupid tune, the same way Roseanne Barr's crotch grab did that time she butchered the

Star Spangled Banner before a nationally-televised ballgame. Each in their own way, Bill Whitman and Roseanne were genius.

I didn't keep going to the Vienna Ceili very long, maybe a year or two. But in the long run, it was a good thing I did. In addition to Bill Whitman and the ubiquitous Jesse Winch on drums, the band at that dance included a fiddler named Joe DeZarn. Joe is, along with Doc Botzer, probably the most generous and welcoming musician in the whole Washington area. And because Joe actually lives way out in Winchester, I extend my definition of the Washington area to include him. Guest musicians were always welcome to sit in with the band at the Vienna Ceili, whether they were good players or not. I never played with the band in Vienna, but once the ceili moved to a hall beside the police station in Fairfax and the band became known as the Bogwanderers, I became a fixture every month as a sit-in. When I started, I really couldn't play at all, but they welcomed me nonetheless. Especially Joe. Eventually I got good enough that they were willing to let me bring my own microphone and plug it into the board (meaning that the dancers might actually hear what I was playing) and they would even let me come and sit in with them when they did "road" gigs at other local ceilis. It was through playing with Joe and another friend who eventually became part of that band, accordionist Danny Flynn, that I learned most of what I know about playing for dancers.

The Blackthorn Stick Ceili was at the same time the most precise in its insistence on proper dancing form and the most family-oriented of all. Both of these traits probably had most to do with the group having been around so long. Multiple generations of families found themselves dancing from the same bible of 32 "approved" dances over the course of several decades. Add in the fact that most all of them were Catholic and it's no accident that the sense of ceremony and tightly-defined ritual were paramount. Just as (in theory, anyway) the Catholic Mass is a social gathering of God's people centered around a series of ritualistic mini-ceremonies like the Creed, the Agnus Dei and the Consecration, the Blackthorn Stick Ceili was a social gathering of God's favorite people – the Irish Americans – centered around a series of dances like the High Cauld Cap, the Sixteen Hand Reel and the Gates of Derry. Just as the faithful at Mass are expected to know the complete order of events without prompting (when the priest says *Dominus vobiscum,* that means he's forgotten the Pope's phone number, so you remind him it's *Et cum spiri two two oh* – even if you have to remind yourself by sneaking a peek in the missal you were given at First Communion) the dancers at the Blackthorn Stick Ceili did not have the benefit of a dance caller to guide them through the intricate figures of whichever of the 32 dances were chosen from the lectionary that night. If they happened to be carrying a copy of *Ar Rinci Foirne* in their back pocket, they could grab a quick refresher. But otherwise, eight bars after the *tap tap* from the drummer it was off to the races for the next eight or ten or even fifteen minutes, and they were on their own for the duration of the dance.

Surprisingly, many of the Blackthorn dancers knew these dances by heart and there were always enough of them in any particular set to guide the whole group through without it all disintegrating. And just as at Mass there are certain parts of the ceremony like the Sign of Peace or the Our Father that are inclusive of even raw beginners, the Blackthorn folks always made sure to have several dances like the Gay Gordons and Shoe the Donkey on the program so that *everyone* could get out on the floor a couple times. As the coup de grace on the whole event, even though the dancers could arrive in mufti for the monthly celebration of the ceili, the Blackthorn Stick's band was required to vest themselves in a uniform in order to mount the stage, just as the priest and altar boys vest themselves to mount the altar. And for the Blackthorn band, that vesting was literal – a green vest worn over a white shirt with black pants. Once vested and ensconced on stage, the Blackthorn band would read the same tunes they played each and every month for years from sheet music elaborately laid out on music stands, just as the priest makes elaborate ceremony of reading the same words at every mass from a book held by an altar boy standing ramrod straight in front of him. This made the Blackthorn Stick Ceili Band at best half authentic – for while I've seen many ceili bands in Ireland that dress alike, I've never seen a one that would use sheet music. They wouldn't be caught dead doing that. Indeed, you could probably assemble a ceili band of disinterred Irish musicians and they'd make better music without sheet music than the Blackthorn band made with it. But the Blackthorn Stick Ceili was never about the music anyway, so that wouldn't bother them in the least.

The family aspect of the Blackthorn group was epitomized by the Stohlman family. Dr. and Mrs. Stohlman, of the same generation as my own parents, were around at the inception of the Blackthorn Stick, and all of their many children (ten, I think, although I never met them all so I don't have an accurate count) were part of the group as they grew up. Those that still lived in the area were likely to show up at the monthly ceili, even if they didn't dance any more. But two of the younger wave of Stohlman kids, Barry and Clare, were even as young adults the best dancers of the lot. It's typical of Irish ceilis for dancers to mix it up and not stick with the same partner all night, but there are always frequent pairings that emerge with husbands and wives or, in the case of Barry and Clare, brother and sister. When the two of them took to the floor together for a dance, it was an event. They both had the perfect build for dancing, tall and thin, and with the natural grace they got from being children of dancers and the many years of dancing together, they moved as one on the floor. And if they were dancing beside you or across from you in a set, you didn't even need to listen to the music because Barry was tapping the rhythms perfectly with his feet, be they the traditional threes-and-sevens of a ceili dance or the distinctive reel, jig, slide or polka of a country set. Barry and Clare seemed to be at every ceili I went to when I started dancing, so they quickly became icons of the scene to me. When Barry moved to Italy to marry his exchange-student girlfriend instead of coming home from the GWCC's epic trip to Dublin in January 1990, it was a foreshadowing of Matt Shortridge leaving the session scene for Wisconsin fifteen or so years later. Things went on, but they were never quite the same or anywhere near as good.

Folks like me who wanted to do the new-fangled set dancing (which actually is older and more traditional than ceili dancing – but don't tell that to the commission) weren't really catered to by the Blackthorn Stick, but they didn't mind if four or eight of us went off to a corner of the floor and danced a set while they were doing the Sixteen Hand Reel or the Haymaker's Jig or some other such lengthy dance. So we did, and since we were never able to get through all the figures of a set before the ceili dance was over, the local set dancing community was always weaker on the later figures of sets than we were on the beginnings. But hey, that's okay – after all, it's better to have danced and had your set collapse than never to have danced at all. But even with stolen moments of set dancing off to the side, there was still a lot of time left to fill at a Blackthorn Ceili if you didn't know their other dances, so myself and a few others started going to their Monday night class in Bethesda to learn them. That is where I learned the so-called threes and sevens, the fundamental step of ceili dancing that somehow manages to work itself out evenly in a music that's based on eight bar phrases. (Even the best dancers have trouble telling their right foot from their left, so how can you expect their math to make sense?) It was at those Monday Blackthorn classes that I first met Kathy O'Rourke, who was then a student at Georgetown University and had discovered Irish dancing after her parents joined the Blackthorn group. Or maybe it was the other way around and she found it first and dragged them into it. I never knew. But Kathy was a natural at the dancing and had been pulled from the pack to demonstrate the threes and sevens and the rising step and all the other exotic moves that the rest of the class needed to master. She became one of my favorite dance partners both before and after she met and eventually married one of my favorite fiddlers, the aforementioned Matt Shortridge. So when they moved to Wisconsin, the loss to the DC Irish scene was a whole lot greater than the sum of its parts.

When the rigors of the dance class were over each Monday, several of us had the habit of going to a nearby basement pub called Flanagan's to unwind. There we were exposed to the second tier of Irish pub singers, since of those that were actually able to cobble together a living by singing their way around the pub circuit Monday was their only night off. One of the "replacement" singers we saw at Flanagan's a lot was a real favorite among all the women in my little group, who absolutely swooned over him. A nice young man called Martin O'Malley, he was then just a guy with a guitar. But after a few years he was able to put together a band called O'Malley's March, complete with uileann pipes, fiddle, accordion and drums, that became quite well known and successful playing Celtic rock. Never successful enough for him to quit the day job, though. Fortunately a few years later Baltimore needed a mayor and then Maryland needed a governor and he was able to stay off the dole.

The tradition of going out after the Monday night Blackthorn Stick dance classes lived on long after I quit going to those classes, and eventually it moved away from Flanagan's. After I had quit dancing and started to try my hand at playing in sessions, several of my old friends from the Blackthorn Stick would come to Nanny O'Brien's late on Monday night to listen to the session and have a pint. Among them were Sue Casey, who lived not far from the pub, and Clare Stohlman. Eventually Clare was accompanied by a man from Dublin who had become her beau, Ray Langley. Ray knew I had once been a set dancer and was now struggling to learn how to play the music, and when I'd pass him on my way out at the end of the night he always had a word of encouragement for me. That meant a lot to me, because I wasn't getting much encouragement at the time and Ray was not only an actual Irishman but one who also knew the music well. Ray and Clare went on to get married a few years later, but then things turned sad when he contracted ALS and eventually succumbed to that disease in 2003, leaving behind Clare and their two young children. Ray's memory lives on through them and through the fundraising walk that their friend Sue Collins spearheads every fall for the ALS Association. And as long as I play the flute I will remember how he encouraged me when I was starting out.

While going to the Blackthorn events and dancing the ceili dances was a lot of fun, they never managed to get me to convert from the new religion I'd gotten, which was to dance the old country sets. First came the Kerry Set, the gateway drug that soon enough led to the great reel sets of Clare like the Caledonian, the Lancers and the Plain. The Plain Set, once I first learned it, quickly became my favorite of all. I could dance it once (or even more) a night for a year and never tire of it. In fact, I think I had a streak going for a year or more of dancing it at least once a week. Just like the pint of plain that is justly celebrated wherever in the world Guinness has reached, the set called Plain is far from that. And it's at its best on a great floor, like the one at the Kennedy-Warren. But long before I'd had the chance to let that knowledge really set in, disaster struck when the management of that building decided to turn their ballroom into a supper club and the GWCC was booted out. (Apparently the potluck suppers we served at all our ceilis didn't earn us any bonus points in the negotiations that never really happened anyway.) This began the persistent search for floor space that defined the rest of my time in the Greater Washington Ceili Club. (Again with the architecture.)

Having danced at so many other ceilis in the Washington area, the rest of the GWCC Board and I knew what kind of dance spaces were out there. There's something about Irish dancing that makes it a less than desirable tenant for dance halls, even though as far as I know the rent has never failed to be paid and dancers (unlike musicians) tend to drink water rather than intoxicants at ceilis, so no halls were ever trashed. (The exception to that rule about dancers drinking water is champion step dancers. I got to know a lot of them when we had them perform at the Irish Festivals at Glen Echo and Wolf Trap, and I quickly learned that if you were trying to find missing stepdancers, the first place to look was always the bar. Perhaps they need that elbow-bending to compensate for all the time spent dancing with their arms tucked rigidly at their side.) The GWCC Ceili was not alone in losing its hall. It soon seemed like every ceili in the area was nomadic, having to move from one hall to another constantly. I remember the Blackthorn Stick holding their monthly dance next to a swimming pool for a while, with the humid, chlorine-soaked atmosphere requiring sweaty dancers like me to bring even more extra shirts than normal. So finding a hall to replace the Kennedy-Warren – never mind a *good* hall – proved quite problematic for the GWCC. An additional complication placed on our search was club president Diana Jensen's insistence that the hall not be too far from her house, which was just across the DC line in Bethesda. For purposes of hosting a monthly dance, we had become the Inside the Beltway Ceili Club.

The GWCC's monthly dance bounced around to several different halls around the area for the first couple of years after we were kicked out of the Kennedy-Warren. We had to change the day to Saturday night to get into some of them, which meant we had to eliminate the potluck supper that was one of the things that made the GWCC Ceili unique. I can't recall the sequence of halls, but I remember there was one at Trinity College where we danced for a while. The low point was probably when Diana got us into a Presbyterian church that was right around the corner from her house. When we went to check it out beforehand, they had a nice hall that had some real possibility. But the night of our first ceili there, we showed up to find out that they had double-booked the nice room and our dance was being relegated to a side room that was about the size of an elementary school classroom. The lady who showed us in was especially proud of it, saying they had just put a new coat of wax on the floor. Of course it was rock-hard linoleum on concrete, the worst possible floor for dancers to batter on. The room might have been okay for eighty or so kids to dance, but we were adults who took up more room. In some cases, a *lot* more room.

And we had a band with trap drum set to fit in there too. When Billy McComiskey, who happened to be playing in the band that night, walked in he took one look around the room and said *Shitty hall. It's gonna be a* great *dance.* And you know what? He was right! Even though by the end of the evening we were all coated with dust from the cloud that rose up as that brand new coat of wax was pulled off the floor by all of our swinging and housing around.

This was perhaps the first example I saw of a strange phenomenon that afflicts (or maybe enhances) Irish music and dancing: The worse the conditions, the better the event. The pattern was to play itself out again and again for the GWCC over the years, perhaps reaching its apex when hurricane-spawned deluges covered our Irish Festival while great music was played for small crowds huddled in tents surrounded by seas of mud. So confident did we become at the inevitability of this phenomenon that we decided to expand our set dancing brand to two spots well outside the greater Washington area, Cape May and Buffalo Gap.

Ron and Diana Jensen had been vacationing at Cape May in New Jersey for several years when they approached the GWCC Board with the idea of doing an "away weekend" there. The Blackthorn Stick had been doing such weekends for a while, usually someplace in the mountains on Halloween. Since the Blackthorn was such a multi-generational family-oriented group, these weekends were a great opportunity for everyone to get away for a while, dress up in costumes, and have some family fun. Sort of like going to Grandma's house, if everyone you knew had the same Grandma. Dancing and music were afterthoughts at the Blackthorn away weekends. In fact, if I remember right from the one time I went, they danced to recorded music. No need to pay their band for an extra gig. But that concept of an away weekend was something that would never work for the GWCC, since dancing and music were basically the only reason the group got together in the first place. Going on a GWCC weekend away where dancing and music weren't the primary focus would be like having your job require you to go on one of those all-hands off-site team-building retreats that every bad manager in the world thinks is a brilliant idea to save his company from abysmal failure. Without the Sword of Lost Paycheck hanging overhead, no one would *ever* attend something like that. (Except for the brown nosers, er, "team players", that is.) We all knew that a GWCC away weekend, in order to succeed, would have to take what we were already doing at our monthly ceilis and ratchet it up a notch. Actually, several notches – and with multiple ratchets involved. Before we really knew what we were getting into, *big* plans were being hatched.

Cape May is a beach town, but not your typical beach town. Its main claim to fame is not its boardwalk or its surf or its loose liquor laws, like so many other beaches, but rather its architecture. (Again with the architecture.) It is possibly the nation's chief depository of authentic Victorian style, thanks to the whole place having been leveled by fire and then rebuilt in the Victorian era. Most of its grand houses, restaurants, hotels and B&Bs had been lovingly and painstakingly restored and kept up over the eighty or so years since, but unfortunately we couldn't afford *those* accommodations, even at the offseason rates. No worries, though, because Diana and Ron had found for us a grand edifice right next to the ocean called Congress Hall. It was in fact Cape May's oldest hotel. Within its premises was a grand foyer that would double as a ballroom for the dance workshops and ceilis during the weekend, it had rooms enough to house the hundred or so dancers we hoped to attract, and a wonderful restaurant that would serve three delicious meals a day for the lot of us. It all sounded grand when they described it to us at the board meeting, except for one thing. Wasn't the place a bit…old? Perhaps a bit…run down? Diana assured us that would not be an issue. Indeed she had a short descriptor for the place that was designed to ease our minds. "Faded elegance." Now how bad could that be?

We were soon to find out. We booked Joe and Siobhan O'Donovan – who had been the big hit of the first Glen Echo Irish Festival GWCC produced in 1986 and were planning a second grand tour of the Irish dancing hotbeds of America for Fall 1988 – as our dance teachers. A happy coincidence of that booking was that Joe O'Donovan's 70$^{th}$ birthday would fall during the weekend and we could celebrate it at Cape May. We engaged our regular ceili band Celtic Thunder, and to have an excuse to bring the singers with them, and also to pull in some extra funds to pay them, we planned a concert for Saturday afternoon that we hoped might pull in a few curious beach walkers at ten bucks a head. Flyers were produced, notices were sent out. Registrations began coming in, and at each monthly board meeting treasurer Suzanne McMenamin would hand out copies of a computer printout showing monies that would be coming in from registrants and going out to the hotel, the band and assorted other entities. I could never make head nor tail of any of them, Suzanne not being an actual accountant and having her own unique system of annotating things, but it seemed like everything was on the up-and-up and we wouldn't be losing money on the deal. The one move we had made, almost as an afterthought, that in retrospect insured the event would at least break even was to pass notice of it to Paul Keating, one of the head honchos of Irish dancing in New York City. It turned out that there wasn't enough interest among the motley collection of dancers within GWCC to fully subscribe an away event, but because Joe and Siobhan had become popular in New York on their first tour, and because most of the members of Celtic Thunder had New York roots, and because it was an easy drive down the Garden State Parkway to Cape May we ended up filling out our allotment of rooms in Congress Hall with about half New Yorkers and half Washingtonians.

The weekend was a resounding success. Beautiful sunny weather that made us feel guilty sitting inside listening to Celtic Thunder and dancing on the lobby floor – a floor that was surprisingly good, albeit a bit small for all of us unless we expanded into the several nooks and crannies that lined its sides. But having to go around the house without smashing into an eighty year old column right next to where you formed your set was good training for us Yank dancers who never had the chance to dance the sets in the tiny thatched roof cottages where those dances were nurtured. We did learn (as most of us had already suspected) that "faded elegance" was Diana-speak for "dilapidated." Paul Keating learned that the hard way when a faded chunk of his room's ceiling fell elegantly down upon his thankfully unoccupied bed. Fortunately he did not hold that against us and continued to help us promote our activities to the New York crowd. But what few bad things happened that weekend paled when put up against the collective improvement in our dancing after exposure to the pure drop teaching of the O'Donovans, and the networking connections with the New Yorkers that were made on and off the dance floor. Indeed, the first Cape May Set Dancing Weekend was such a triumph that it went to our heads. It emboldened us. And the next thing we knew, we were planning to try the whole thing again at a place called Buffalo Gap.

I can't remember what the connection was that put us on to Buffalo Gap, although like almost every other grand scheme the GWCC ever had I know Mike Denney was in on it somehow. I had heard of the place, had seen flyers for contradance weekends there on the back table in the Glen Echo Spanish Ballroom where we had the Wednesday night set dancing classes, but since there really wasn't much overlap between the contradancing crowd and the Irish dance scene I never thought it could become a venue for us. But the owners of the place, who held the DC franchise for something called International Folk Dancing, seemed to think it would be the ideal place for us to do something. And so it was that a small group from the GWCC Board, including me, found ourselves meeting with one of the Buffalo Gap guys at his house – an actual, real life log cabin in Chevy Chase, Maryland, inside the Beltway. Even in 1989, I never would have guessed such a place could exist. I wonder if it's still there now? As it turned out, this log cabin was but a foreshadowing of what we would encounter at Buffalo Gap, which was a former kids camp located in the West Virginia hills just across the state line from northern Virginia, a short two hour drive from DC. As it was explained to us, the International Folk Dancing crowd – who espoused internationality about as much as the baseball World Series does, since all their dances seemed to come from either eastern Europe or Scandinavia – had been conducting highly successful dance weekends there on Memorial Day and Labor Day for years. Other dance groups used the place for weeks or weekends devoted to contradancing, English Country Dancing and the like. GWCC was looking to expand its away weekends, with Mike Denney thinking grand thoughts as always and hoping there could be two or three such weekends each year to go along with the spring Washington Irish Festival as showcase events for the club. Cape May of course would continue in the fall, and for summer we could add a weekend at Buffalo Gap.

The planets did all seem to be aligning for an epic event. Mick Moloney's Augusta Irish Week in West Virginia had already booked Joe and Siobhan O'Donovan for the next July and was expanding to include musicians and stepdancers from Cape Breton and Quebec. The Buffalo Gap Camp was available for the weekend prior to that, so all of them could come there for a true multi-traditional weekend of music and dance before traveling two hours on the winding roads to Elkins for Mick's week. The camp offered not one, but two dance halls, cabin space for a couple hundred people, a dining hall with a chef supposedly renowned for great cuisine, a swimming pond, and acres of gorgeous mountain land. By the time we said our goodbyes that night to your man in the log cabin, the wheels were well in motion, subject to a site visit that would be set up for us at some point. Almost lost in all the excitement of the evening was his statement that we'd need to develop our "sauna policy" for the event. In apparent solidarity with the Scandinavian traditions of sauna – which from what I can tell are much more enduring than their dance and music traditions – the Buffalo Gap Camp had installed such a facility. And in solidarity with the Scandinavian tradition (or so we were told) camp attendees typically used the facility in the European manner, in which clothing was superfluous, indeed forbidden, what with all the heat in there. This was well before Ireland joined up with the continent to form the magnificent European Union, and Al Gore had yet to tell us the globe was inconveniently warming around us. We were well aware that there's one thing folks from Ireland know about heat: there's not enough of it to go around. So when it comes to clothes, you put them on rather than take them off. If an Irish crowd was going to spend a weekend in close proximity with a sauna, rules and disclaimers and warnings had best be at the ready to avoid any unfortunate occurrences or awkward encounters with too much flesh.

Just as we had done with Cape May, the bulk of the GWCC Board signed off on the Buffalo Gap weekend and ventured well into the planning of it without ever having seen the place. For Cape May the palliative words that were meant to ease our fear of the unknown had been "faded elegance"; for Buffalo Gap the operative descriptor of the site that was meant to do the same was "cozy." Our initial visit to this camp in the mountains, some five months after that first meeting in your man's log cabin – and well beyond the point of no return – revealed that "cozy" was naught but a smokescreen for "ramshackle." Aside from the tin roof on the largest dance hall (which was actually a basketball court, not a dance hall – befitting the place's inception as a kids camp) every building on the lot was made entirely of wood. The sauna building and a covered pavilion built into the side of a hill were the sturdiest of them all, indeed the only ones that could be called sturdy at all. They had both been recently built by a North Carolina mountain man who also taught a class in log cabin construction at Augusta each summer. (It was always interesting during Irish Week to watch a log cabin rise on campus in inverse process of how we Irish Week students and staff were decaying as a result of our long nights filled with tunes, drink and assorted bonhomie.)

The rest of the buildings at Buffalo Gap reminded me of the many old barns I had seen along the roads in West Virginia as my family drove back to my grandmother's farm in the summers of my childhood. Each year that we passed them, what paint was left on their sides had faded some more, and another several boards had fallen off their walls. I'd wonder each time we passed one why it hadn't fallen down yet. The only thing different about the Buffalo Gap buildings was that they didn't have "Chew Mail Pouch Tobacco" ads painted on their sides like the old barns did. We had christened our new event The First Annual GWCC Crossroads Ceili Weekend, in a nod both to the mix of music and dance cultures we were featuring and to the place in rural Ireland where dances used to occur. The country folk in Ireland had danced outside at the crossroads because the tiny cottages where they lived didn't provide adequate space inside for dancers and musicians to move. The irony was totally lost on us that we would now be asking people in the modern day to come and help revive the old dance styles while sleeping and eating in facilities that might well have been *worse* than those endured in the backward times when those dances were new.

One of the sleeping cabins at Buffalo Gap was divvied up into individual rooms complete with indoor plumbing; that one was quickly designated as quarters for the dance teachers and musicians who would be staffing the weekend. Another cabin or two had the semblance of private rooms with shared toilet and shower facilities in the building, and those of us on the planning committee quickly reserved our spots therein. But the bulk of the cabins featured large rooms full of bunks, befitting an Army barracks. All of them at least had indoor toilets, but over half of them had no shower facilities, instead requiring their residents to schlep outside to a cinder block building to wash up. The camp's owners claimed it had a capacity of 300, but with that many people it would have resembled the workhouses where the poor clung to life during the Great Hunger – definitely not what the ancestors of our hoped-for attendees would have had in mind for their great-grandchildren when they were riding the coffin ships over to America.

Fortunately our weekend was not subscribed heavily enough to fill out the camp to the max. Perhaps word got out on what was waiting there and scared some people off. Whatever the reason, we ended up with about 100 people at the first Crossroads Ceili Weekend, so at least everyone had a little personal space to spread out when they weren't playing or dancing, even though it was far from ideal.

In refreshing my memory of events that took place over 20 years ago, I recently rummaged through a stack of old papers in my unorganized basement archive and discovered an actual list of attendees to that weekend at Buffalo Gap. We had people from as far away as Chicago, Massachusetts and New York in addition to the expected folks from the DC-Baltimore ceili scene. Many of the names looked familiar to me, most as folks I knew back then but had not seen for years. One name jumped out at me, though: Jane Sullivan of Washington DC. That happens to be the name of the wife of the current Chief Justice of the Supreme Court, John Roberts, and would seem to be nothing more than coincidence – except for the Chief Justice himself having been revealed recently as a closet Irish set dancer who came to the dancing *via his wife*. Could that be the same Jane Sullivan who learned Irish sets from Joe and Siobhan O'Donovan at Buffalo Gap one weekend in July 1989? I'll never know, and unless she and her husband repeat their visit to a local session sometime, I won't be able to ask. But I like to think that if it was the same woman, the memories that were charred upon her brain that weekend of how people of otherwise high upbringing are sometimes forced through no fault of their own to spend time in virtual hovels might have helped convince her husband that health care for all is not such a bad idea after all. Or maybe it was some other Jane Sullivan and she's spent the ensuing decades vowing never to go near anything involving Irish music or dancing ever again.

There was only one promise made by your man at the log cabin meeting that did eventually pan out. The food at Buffalo Gap was indeed awesome, and as a bit of a cook myself I enjoyed hanging out in the kitchen with their chef and seeing how a meal for 100 gets put together. Unfortunately, all 100 of our campers didn't enjoy what got put on their plates after our little committee was done consulting with the chef on menu choices. As was our habit from GWCC Board and committee meetings over the years, we went eclectic. At meetings we were likely to have Pad Thai or Indian curry or whichever other exotic carryout was nearby. No Domino's pizza for us! Once we heard that the Buffalo Gap chef could prepare stuff like that we just assumed that everyone who came to our weekend would share our exquisitely adventurous palate. Boy, were we wrong. And the ones who really paid the price for that were our honored guests, our staff of musicians and dance teachers from foreign lands. Lands whose own cuisines had migrated to white bread middle America, far from where we wanted to be. Natalie MacMaster, the teenage fiddler from Cape Breton, had no idea what a taco was until a platter full of shells and make-your-own fixins was plopped on her table, family style, for Saturday lunch. Poor Siobhan O'Donovan, who served me massive fry-ups every time I visited her and Joe in Cork, was spotted at dinner on Saturday night with just a roll on her plate. For our esteemed visitors from Ireland, we had reproduced not only the living conditions of the Great Hunger, but the Great Hunger itself!

To take their minds off the food, we worked the staff like dogs. Dance workshops with live music from nine in the morning until noon, and again for three hours in the afternoon. Then the concert, a dinner break and the grand evening ceili. With the highest heat and humidity of the entire summer descending on Buffalo Gap that weekend, it's a miracle everyone survived, with not even one casualty. Brendan Mulvihill emerged from fiddling for Joe and Siobhan's afternoon dance class in the tin-roofed basketball arena – basically a giant EZ-Bake Oven – and likened the conditions to working in the salt mines. Since I was on the floor dancing during that workshop, I know he wasn't exaggerating – even though there are no salt mines anywhere near Birmingham, England or The Bronx, where Brendan lived before coming to DC, where I grew up and where there also aren't any salt mines. Joe and Siobhan – the two septuagenarians who we billed on our flyer as *Direct from Ireland*, a land that knows not of air conditioning or the oppressive heat that makes it necessary – never once complained through it all. But that may have been because they were too busy saying the rosary in grateful thanks for not keeling over dead from heat stroke or a heart attack. And to think we went through that entire weekend with nary the thought of taking out any kind of insurance policy – or if we did think of it, we quickly dismissed the idea since we'd never have been able to pay the premium. I don't know if God exists, but if he does he was definitely on our side that weekend.

While the conditions at Buffalo Gap were substandard, the music and dance that emerged there were out of this world. Men and women mingled all weekend on the dance floor and throughout the camp while our carefully crafted sauna policy prevented any occurrences of eyeballs being offended by too much exposed flesh of the opposite sex. (Actually one transgression along those lines did occur, so I heard, but it was outside the sauna. On Sunday, one of the advance people from the Balkan dance group who would be using the camp during the following week arrived, and she decided to take a shower. Not realizing that the two cinderblock shower huts had been designated for men only or women only rather than coed as the Balkans like, she walked right in on one of our male dancers as he was lathering up. Since this kind of thing never happens to me, alas, I don't know if he should have been offended or not. But I don't recall hearing any complaints.) Billy McComiskey's *Shitty hall. Gonna be a* great *dance* theory had once again proved true at our Buffalo Gap weekend. But without even trying, we had established the lower bound of architecture that would support an Irish set dancing event. (Again with the architecture.) Not precisely, though. All we knew was that whatever that lower bound was, it was somewhere *above* Buffalo Gap. Your man in the log cabin and his comrades would have gladly hosted the Second, Third and All Successive Annual GWCC Crossroads Ceili Weekends throughout eternity, but it was not to be. We did try again the next July at a different, more upscale facility near Luray Caverns called Mimslyn, but after that we lost our connection with Cape Breton and Quebecois dancing when Augusta quit bringing folks down from there. A strictly Irish dancing weekend at Mimslyn would have been like doing another Cape May Weekend without the ocean, and so it came to be that the weekend in the Land of Faded Elegance has survived until today, while the Ceili Crossroads in the mountains was closed forever.

During the whole time I was obsessed with Irish set dancing, there was something that always differentiated me from the rest of the crowd, and after three or four years of spending every other night on a dance floor that difference began to manifest itself. (No, the difference wasn't that I sweat a lot more than most dancers do and therefore need to carry a larger duffel bag full of clothing with me when I'm out dancing – although that *is* true.) I noticed early on that most other dancers weren't really listening to the music other than to get the beat and move to it. They would have been just as happy (or almost, anyway) dancing to the beat of a drummer rather than a full band. In the age old debate over which came first, the dancing or the music, they were all on the side of the dance – while I, in contrast, found dancing to be like the Wizard of Oz. When I started dancing, having never done so in my youth, everything was in black and white. I was totally focused on getting the step down, learning how to shift my weight, and figuring out how to move in concert with my partner through all the many figures of all the many sets I was learning. Eventually, that all became natural to me and I stepped into a world of color, realizing there was music all around me. Music that I liked. Music that I liked *a lot*. Music that I *wanted to play*. Somewhere along that way, I bought a flute, and further along that way I realized that if I was ever going to be able to play it I needed to be doing that in the evenings rather than heading out to a dance class or a ceili.

So that's why I quit dancing. Either that, or I was getting tired of all the architecture hassles that dancing required. Music can be played practically anywhere, which is why Frank Zappa didn't say that writing about dancing is like playing a tune about architecture. If you're a musician, one set of clothes a day is plenty. (For some musicians, one set of clothes is enough for *several* days – but I'm not going there.) Feet can be tapped no matter what shoes are on them or what floor is beneath them. As I transitioned out of dancing, there was less and less reason for me to remain in the GWCC or on its board. But since the club did still run the Irish Festival, I hung around as a member until the festival died, and before I left I came up with a couple of ideas that are still paying dividends for them now – and both of them involved architecture. (Again...)

The first of my brilliant ideas did take a while to catch on. While the club was still in its years of exile from the Kennedy-Warren Ballroom, wandering the desert in search of a dance floor for the monthly ceili, I was wandering myself through different styles of dance on nights I wasn't dancing Irish. One night at a Cajun dance, I happened to step onto a floor that was perfect. Near where two of DC's biggest highways come together to form one of its biggest traffic jams sat a campground for vagabond tourists looking for a place to park their Winnebagos while they visit the Nation's Capital Stuck in the middle of it was a building that served as its community center. Sited next to a swimming pool, the bottom floor of this building held the requisite washing machines, snack bar and other amenities campers look for. But on the second floor, incongruously, was a large room with one side full of windows, a fireplace in the corner, and a sprung hardwood dance floor. With ample free parking right outside the door, the place was perfect for a ceili. It had the oddity factor going for it too, with the view right out the window of a sea of what basically are the American equivalent of Irish caravans, with their inhabitants doing all their cooking and drying of laundry right outside their front doors. Even the price was right. There was only one thing wrong with the place – it was too far from Diana Jensen's house. So it took several more years of continued wandering before all other options were exhausted, and at last my idea didn't look so bad after all. The GWCC has been holding its ceili there ever since. Must be over 15 years now.

The other legacy I left for GWCC was born less from brilliant brainwork on my part than from loneliness and boredom. As a single guy I was short of options for New Year's Eve and looking at a future of sitting at home watching the ball come down on TV. I've never been one for hitting the crowded bar scene, but had been to a couple of New

Year's Eve contradances that were kind of fun. I thought *Why not have a ceili on New Year's Eve?* When I brought my idea to the board, they didn't laugh in my face. Instead they said sure, we'll do it – as long as you do all the work. So I was off, as I recall without even a committee to help me out. As it turned out, all my problems ended up being architectural. (Again…) The simple solution would have been to transfer all aspects of the regular December GWCC Ceili to New Years Eve, technically still a day in December. But that was complicated by the fact that neither the regular band nor the ballroom were available that night, Celtic Thunder having another longstanding gig and the Kennedy-Warren scoffing at the pittance we paid to rent the space on otherwise useless late Sunday afternoons being adequate for them to close their doors to all the high rollers in search of places to spend their money on New Year's Eve.

Finding another band proved easy. Even then, with the scene being nowhere near as mature as it is now, there were always more quality Irish musicians chasing gigs than there were gigs to support them. Brendan Mulvihill, Donna Long and Zan McLeod quickly agreed to play on New Year's Eve at a price only slightly more than it would have taken to get them for a regular monthly ceili. With that settled, I embarked on an all-out search for a venue. With no Internet or Google available then, I had to rely on a guidebook I had found of interesting places in the DC area for wedding receptions. That was close enough, for what is a ceili anyway but a wedding reception where no one has to make a commitment that will end up costing them either their lifetime or a huge chunk of money and massive legal hassle? Music, dance, food, drink, relatives and friends, it's all the same. Maybe you don't need to spring for a ceili cake, but on New Year's Eve there still needs to be champagne. As it turned out, that would be the big hurdle with the facility I found that looked most promising – an old Grange building on the western edge of the Washington suburbs that had been fixed up and was being run as a park by the county. It was a sturdy facility with a great sprung wood floor and a stage for the band. A bit smaller than our regular floor, but the acceptable increase in admission fee for a holiday event would offset a smaller crowd and still leave us enough cash to rent the place for the evening. Aside from their no-alcohol policy, the county's only other sticking point was that an event that went past midnight would keep the site's caretaker up past her bedtime.

Having worked in an earlier life at a different park in the county, where my ranger boss drove his truck around the park with a six pack on the seat next to him (it was a far simpler time 40 years ago) I knew that a no-alcohol policy could be treated the same as the 55 mile an hour speed limit – merely a suggestion. And sure enough, I was able to convince park management that we were dancers, not drinkers (that was the truth as well, which made it easier) and we were allowed enough champagne for a toast at midnight. The caretaker agreed to stay up late, as long as we were out by 12:30. We were in! And when the festive night had come and gone, it seemed to us that it had gone off without a hitch. Oh, there was the small matter of the caretaker being scared out of her wits by the sound of all the battering feet hitting the floor that was also the ceiling above her office, and her taking refuge in a nearby outbuilding lest the floor cave in on her head. But the building was so sturdily built that when she came back at precisely half twelve to lock the door behind us as we left, there was no sign on either the floor or the ceiling beams below that we had ever been there. So I felt supremely confident when I rang the county park office bright and early on the very next business day to book the facility again for the following year, only to be told that a new policy had been adopted. Apparently there had been some overtime put in over the weekend by the park staff, and the new rule that emerged was *No New Year's Eve events.* Although I didn't verbalize it at the time, I immediately saw this for what it was. It had taken an entire committee of us to re-create the Great Hunger at Buffalo Gap. Here I had resurrected No Irish Need Apply all on my own.

But unlike the First and Last Annual GWCC Crossroads Ceili Weekend, the GWCC New Year's Eve Ceili lived on. After an interval of a few years, it was revived, and continues to take place today at that very same campground dance hall I first recommended to the board. I doubt that anyone currently involved in the Washington Irish ceili scene even knows that they have me to thank for that facility and that event, but that's okay. There aren't even many people around who remember that I was once a dancer. There really isn't all that much overlap between the Irish dance and Irish music communities, at least not in Washington. Dancers know the musicians who play at the ceili and at the feis, and musicians who are lucky enough to play at a ceili or unlucky enough to play at a feis know the dancers. Otherwise, it seems we live our lives in parallel streams. Every so often I have the chance to sit in with the band at one of the local ceilis I used to frequent as a dancer. I wish I could do it more, because I really like playing for dancers. But there are a lot of other musicians around here who like doing that too, and as always there are not enough dances to go around for everyone to have the chance to play. Whenever I do find myself at a ceili, though, and I hear the tap-tap of the wood block that signals the first notes of the tune, I always find myself thinking, for just a moment anyway, that I should be out on the floor. But then I look around and see that none of my old familiar dance partners are there. I look at my feet and realize I'm wearing the wrong kind of shoes, and I remember that I don't have a spare shirt to put on once I sweat through the one I'm wearing. So I pick up the flute and start to play. There's a lot of stuff involved with being a dancer, a lot of requirements it puts on you. Playing music is much, much easier. Once you get past the learning part, that is.

## Learning the Hard Way

The best way to become an Irish traditional musician is to start young, to either be born into a family of players or grow up someplace where there are musicians among your neighbors. That's why it's traditional music, after all, because it's passed down from one generation to the next. So if I had been born a generation sooner than I was, there would have been no chance I could ever play this music, because no one in my family played it and indeed no one anywhere near me (including myself) even knew it existed. I never would have heard Irish traditional music at all. But thanks to the wonders of recordings and radio, I was lucky enough to hear the music when I was in my late twenties, and sometime after I turned 30 I decided I wanted to play it. At least I had a chance.

The second best way to become an Irish traditional musician, no matter your age, is to find a teacher or mentor to show you the way. The music is passed orally and aurally, almost by word of mouth or hearsay. Tunebooks and written material exist, but they are useless on their own to make a musician. Likewise, there are lots of recordings – and were even back in the 1980s when I was starting – but simply listening can only get you so far. Entertainment, enjoyment, excitement at hearing the music come easily, but to truly learn it and make it your own you need someone to tell you or show you how to listen. And if you want to play the music yourself, you need someone who plays the instrument you're trying to learn. This is true whether you already know how to play that instrument in the context of other music or if you've never picked up the instrument before.

When I discovered Irish traditional music, I was lucky that there were local resources where I could get tunebooks and recordings galore. (Big plug here for HMT, a.k.a. the House of Musical Traditions in Takoma Park, Maryland.) When I decided I wanted to play the music on the flute, I was lucky again. I found a keyless flute made by Casey Burns at HMT, messed around with it for a couple of years, and then walked up to the table of Patrick Olwell – probably the greatest maker of wooden flutes who ever lived in America – at the Glen Echo Irish Festival in 1992. Knowing that it took a while on his waiting list to get a flute from him, I asked him how long the wait would be for a keyless. He said *Well, I have this one here that's two weeks short of being done and still not spoken for.* Almost before that sentence was out of his mouth I said *Let me write you a check right now.* Two weeks later, the flute arrived in the mail. (It's a good thing I was lucky that day, because I was way too young to try the Rafferty Gambit, a move perfected by the great Mike Rafferty at that very same spot a few years before. Mike, who had learned the flute the best way as a child in rural Galway, was then undergoing a revival in his playing, having retired from his day job a few years before. But good flutes being hard to find at the time, he was playing a silver flute. He came to Patrick's table at the Glen Echo festival when he was performing there, had a blow on one of the demonstration flutes and loved it. But Patrick told him he couldn't sell it because it was a demo. Mike then asked the same question I later asked, *How long do I have to wait to get a flute?* The answer was six months, to which Mike said *But I could be dead by then!* Patrick had no way to counter that, other than to sell him the flute.)

But even though I had a flute and all the accoutrements, I was still handicapped in my quest to learn the music, since I had no access to a teacher. The closest Irish flute teachers I knew of were Frank Claudy and Chris Norman, both in Baltimore, and that was just too far away for a guy like me with a day job – even in the 1990s when the drive only took an hour even at the height of rush hour and gas was only slightly more than a buck per gallon rather than four. Then I discovered that the third best way to become an Irish traditional musician is to be a dancer first. Not only had my five years of set dancing experience given my body a feel of the rhythm and swing of Irish music, they had introduced me to the concept of a summer school, and two of them in particular. I had become a regular at Mick Moloney's Augusta Irish Week in West Virginia since 1985, and had been over to the Willie Clancy Summer School in County Clare twice, in 1987 and 1991, to take set dancing classes. Now that I had a flute and was learning to play it, it seemed the logical next progression in the sequence was to sign up for the flute class at Augusta in July 1991.

And so it was that I found myself on a Monday morning sitting together with a dozen or so other aspiring flute players in a science classroom on the Davis and Elkins College campus when Jack Coen walked in. He might have said a cursory hello, I don't really recall. He walked up to the counter at the front of the room by the blackboard, where there was a sink that was normally used for cleaning up after science experiments. It had the high inverted U-shaped faucet that would let you put something big under it. Jack took his flute, an old German model wooden one, out of its case and before putting it together he stuck each piece of it under the faucet and ran a healthy stream of water through it. As he did so, he gave us the first words of instruction we would receive from him. *Never, ever do this.*

Jack Coen at the time would have been in his mid sixties, over forty years in America after emigrating as a young man from his native Woodford, Co. Galway to New York. He brought with him to America a way of playing the flute that was often referred to as the East Galway style. Relaxed, steady and melodic, Jack's style was the complete antithesis of what nearly all aspiring Irish flute players were trying to emulate at the time, which was the highly ornamented playing of Matt Molloy and Seamus Egan. Fair play to them, for that kind of playing was what put Irish flute playing on the map in a music that until then had been dominated by pipes, fiddles and accordions. It was exactly what was needed on the stage or in a large session, which was where most people looked for Irish music. Jack Coen's playing, on the other hand, was a throwback to the days when Irish music was played in a rural cottage by family or neighbors gathered around the fire. It was often said by those who analyzed the playing of Irish music that Jack Coen didn't play ornaments, which was basically true. If asked by a student about how to execute ornamentation in a tune he was teaching, Jack would invariably say *You just wiggle your fingers a bit there*. But if you sat next to Jack while he was playing, there were lovely little bits all over the place where he was just wiggling his fingers, and those bits turned the basic notes of the tune into the most sublime music possible. I realized early on in the classes I had with Jack that I wasn't going to be learning flute technique from him. I was going to learn how to make music.

It was welcome learning for me, but the process was slow. I only had access to Jack for one week out of the year for five of those years I was at Augusta. I would leave Elkins at the end of those weeks with cassette tapes full of tunes and a pile of good intentions, armed with one of Jack's choicest bits of wisdom. *Always play with someone who's better than you are. That way you can only get better.* This is where the challenge came in. It wasn't that there were no players better than me at home. Indeed there were plenty of them, but the only real opportunity to play with them was at the local session, which was every Monday night at Nanny O'Brien's. Barring the rare invitation to a house party or other such event, Nanny's was the only game in town, and it was there that I learned that the fourth best way to become an Irish traditional musician is to try to learn at sessions. Sessions are marvelous social opportunities and great places to hear the music and share whatever music you have yourself. But trying to learn Irish music by jumping headfirst into the session scene is like trying to learn biology by jumping into a Petri dish. You never know what's growing in there. It could be good, or it could be bad. Truth be told, when I started going to Nanny's there were a lot more good influences there than there were bad, but it was a big session and it was hard to sort out who to try to take after. Working on the tunes and the style I brought home with me from Jack's class always sooner or later ended up taking a back seat to trying to keep pace with the new tunes that were being thrown at me every Monday night. My hectic urban lifestyle just did not lend itself to absorbing a relaxed, steady and melodic playing style.

Yet I did make progress, slowly but surely. It came as a shock to the system, though, when Jack Coen retired from teaching at Augusta and Seamus Egan took over the next year. Class size ballooned from a dozen or so with Jack to over twenty with Seamus. Everyone there was absolutely obsessed with trying to grab for themselves every single roll, cran, cut, bubble and squeak that Seamus puts into his playing to make it so dynamic and exciting. One guy was so fixated on not missing anything that he constantly asked Seamus if he was doing something with his lip whenever it seemed that replicating the finger work just wasn't enough to make him sound exactly like Seamus. In all, Seamus must have given us close to twenty of his tricks, each of them laid out in painstaking detail. A far cry from Jack's "just wiggle your fingers a bit." In isolation, I could do every single one of them. It was putting them together on top of a tune and having music come out that proved elusive. You can go to the store and buy a grocery list full of ingredients, but that doesn't mean you'll have a delicious dinner. Someone has to be able to cook it, and if the cook can't handle a mix of all the ingredients the best approach is to pare things down to a minimum. Less is more, as Jack Coen intuitively knew and most of the rest of us struggled to realize. While many of my session colleagues were honing their skills – sometimes even with success – on backstitches, double-cut long roles and the like, I pared my toolbox of ornaments down to just cuts, taps, rolls and crans. That helped. But I still had a fatal flaw in my approach. If I heard a new tune at a session or on a recording and I wanted to learn it, the only way I knew how to do it was to find the sheet music somewhere. Old habits bred in my high school band days died very hard.

Six years in from acquiring my prized Olwell flute, my playing had plateaued – and not in a good spot. I made the drastic decision to go to Willie Week and take a flute class. Actually, it wasn't really all that drastic a move. I was overdue for a trip to Ireland, I always tried to build my itineraries around an "event", and I'd been to Willie Week a few times before and it was always good. So, okay, maybe taking flute class there wasn't such a drastic move after all. It was preordained. But there was a big difference between the flute classes at Willie Week and the flute classes I'd been taking at Augusta. You couldn't just pick a class and enroll, you had to audition for a spot. That was something I hadn't had to do since high school band, where I had nerves of steel (or maybe it was just naiveté) and always did well. Such was not the case once I took up Irish music, though, for some reason. Maybe it was because playing music meant more to me now than it did when I was a kid, so I wanted it to be good. And my playing never seemed as good when there was someone else listening as it did when I was alone at home – especially if the listener was listening critically.

The nerves weren't helped at all by the Willie Week auditions not being blind – that is, played behind a screen – like all my high school auditions and competitions had been. Instead, following the instructions laid out at registration, myself and over a hundred other flute players crammed into a single classroom in the National School at 10:00 on the Monday morning. Fortunately they had moved the normal array of small desks out of the way, but it was still a scene that would cause apoplexy in an American fire marshal. But in a nation where they don't even bother with safety railings on the edge of the 600-foot-high Cliffs of Moher, no big deal. Mick Hand, who was in charge of the flute program at Willie Week, came in and eventually managed to silence the cacophony of flute players warming up (what a blessing to not be auditioning for a whistle class!) and barked out the instruction. *If you've been playing two years or less, line up by the door. Two to four years, line up in the middle. More than four years, line up by the windows.* I'd been playing more than four years, so I went over by the window, where I was about twentieth in line. Marcas O Murchu, the Belfast flute player that I knew through his recordings, started working his way down the line. He'd have each person play a bit of a tune, and then he'd tell them what teacher's class they'd go in. For about the first ten, it was *You come with me.* Then Marcas reached an older gentleman, who tried to play but no sound came out of his flute. He regrouped and tried again, but still no sound. Marcas said *Maybe you have a leak. Let me have a blow on it.* Marcas played the flute beautifully, handed it back to the unfortunate gentleman, and said *You go with Catherine McEvoy.*

Marcas continued working his way down the line, with every player being told to come to his class, until finally he got to me. The tune choice was mine to make, and after much internal deliberation as the audition line proceeded I had decided on a jig. I put the flute to my lips and launched into it. I had gotten about halfway into the first part when someone out in the hallway yelled to Marcas and he walked off. When he came back after a minute or so, I asked if I should play again and he said yes. I got maybe two bars further into the tune than I had before, and he said to me *You go with Catherine.* It was not lost on me that the only other flute player Marcas had sent to Catherine's class was the guy who couldn't even get a sound out of his flute. Clearly, Marcas O Murchu's opinion of my flute playing, almost a decade in, was not as high as mine. As it turned out, Marcas was right. And that was how I found out that the fifth best way to become an Irish traditional musician is to find the right role model.

I don't think I knew who Catherine McEvoy was before I ended up in her class in Willie Week that year. I might have heard her name, since she had just put out a CD with Felix Dolan, who I did know from 10 years of Washington Irish Festivals. But I had never heard her play, either live or on that CD, and I knew absolutely nothing about her. Once again, luck had intervened for me, because if given the choice of which class to take that week I never would have picked hers. So as painful as the audition process had been that morning, it put me in the right place. From the moment I sat down on the little bench to learn from Catherine, in another grade school classroom just down the hall from the site of my nightmare audition, something clicked. The light bulb went on for me as a flute player. I can't pin it on any one particular thing, though. It may have had something to do with Catherine being a left-handed player, so that watching her was like looking in a mirror, making technique easier to pick up. It might have been that, unlike other flute players I'd taken class with, Catherine is a music teacher in her day job. And since she teaches blind kids, that puts her in a good place for teaching music that really needs to be learned by ear. (Not to be slagging the other great flute players I'd had classes with, but often the best players are not the best teachers. But equally untrue is the old saying that those who can't do, teach. Catherine McEvoy is that rare combination of brilliant musician and gifted teacher. If she was a man, she'd be a man you don't meet every day. But she's not. And I digress.)

In thinking about it, though, it comes to me that the biggest difference between what happened to me in Catherine's class and what happened in the other classes I had taken before then (and would take after) is that Catherine *made us play*. So many teachers of group music classes are reluctant to do that, probably because they don't want to embarrass one student in front of the others by offering feedback to them. Yet it's the feedback from teacher to student that is the most important part of the relationship, because only so much can be learned by osmosis. The student may think he or she is doing fine, but without a finely honed critical ear of their own they have no way to judge that. And even if they do have one, it's hard for a musician to apply a critical ear to their playing while they're playing. You need to listen to a recording of yourself to really hear how you sound, and when you're trying to learn to play music recording yourself is the last thing you want to do, because it preserves all the mistakes for painful posterity. As I had found out through many years of group classes, it is possible to learn by sitting with a great player who can show you how it's done, either in general like Jack Coen did, or in minute detail like Seamus Egan. But to break through to the next level, you need someone to tell you whether what you are doing is right or wrong, and if you're doing it wrong, tell you what you need to do to make it right. Private teachers do this all the time, either bluntly or with tact. Both approaches work. But to do the same thing in a group setting requires great tact and extreme finesse, which Catherine's experience teaching youngsters had gifted her with. That made learning from her a lot less painful and embarrassing than it could have been, which was a good thing since the large majority of that class at Willie Week was kids under 12 who had only been playing a year or two. Yet they could play rings around me and all the other adults (mostly Yanks) in that class. You can never be too humble when you're an adult trying to learn an age-old tradition.

But it turned out that Catherine wasn't just the right role model for me because she was able to teach me without embarrassing me. Equally important was that she herself wasn't bothered by being followed around – stalked, really – by a group of us from the class. Her Willie Week routine was to wander into town an hour or so after class ended at one o'clock and spend the afternoon playing in a session with a few of her friends, who happened to be some of the greats of Irish music, like fiddlers James Kelly and his older brother John, Brendan McGlinchey, and the legendary Bobby Casey. They would play in a pub on the Ennis Road, just on the edge of where the townland of Miltown Malbay met the pastures of County Clare. Actually, for the first couple of summers I was stalking her around Miltown, they didn't even play in the pub proper, they played in the kitchen just off the pub, which the publican had opened up for the week to accommodate the crowds. In the evenings, every pub in Miltown would be packed to the gills, with an auxiliary mob outside the door pushing to get in, which made it impossible to hear or play any music. But in the afternoons, things were much more manageable. I was able to get a seat on the fringe of Catherine's session and see how the music she was teaching us in class is supposed to be played. The tempos were relaxed, not manic like they were in every other Miltown session that week. The tunes flowed organically, an integral part of an ongoing conversation between the players that was as much spoken word as it was music. Everywhere else, a tune was a salvo thrown out in a crowded room to draw attention to the player. *Hey, look at me. I'm here.* Like a voice crying out in the wilderness, except it wasn't a wilderness, it was a mob. Sitting in or near such a session (assuming you could even get a seat) was like walking down a city street in the heat of summer when everyone has their windows open and hearing snippets of the sounds inside as you passed by. It wasn't a musical experience, it was sound bites. In contrast, the sessions I followed Catherine around to were like self-contained participatory performance events, where the tunes were just part of an ongoing musical experience. A community coming together, almost like a church, without the whole God aspect complicating things.

In the sessions where I watched Catherine play at Willie Week, and at the other places I soon found myself following her around – the Gaelic Roots weeks at Boston College, the Friday Harbor Irish Music Camp near Seattle; I was downright bicoastal in my pursuit – I began to see parallels with the sessions I'd experienced at my own local, Nanny O'Brien's, and at other pubs around DC. In the local sessions, the feeling of community was there, even if the music hadn't quite made it yet. But I could see that the seed for the music had been sown there, and that it had been germinating even before I had started going to sessions. That's when I realized that the sixth best way to become an Irish traditional musician is to just throw yourself into it if you're lucky enough to find it, and then to persevere. Jack Coen was right when he said *Always play with someone who's better than you are. That way you can only get better.* But what he didn't say after that is just as important, because it's not always possible to find someone who's better than you are to play with. When that's the case, it's good enough to find others who, like you, are striving to get better. Because even though there are many ways to become an Irish traditional musician, some better than others, there is no way to become one in isolation. If you find a community of musicians that's striving to play in the Irish traditional style, and if you dive in with them and play along, eventually you'll find that you've all become Irish traditional musicians. It may take a long time, but eventually it will happen. And really, that's the only way to become an Irish traditional musician.

Catherine McEvoy at the Willie Clancy
Summer School, July 1998.

# Two Old Black Sticks

It is purely an accident of chance that I play Irish music today – or as I prefer to think of it, extreme good fortune. I do have some Irish in my bloodline. My paternal grandfather Frank Kerr and grandmother Marie Mullen were born in America of Irish immigrant parents, but as best I know there was no feeling of Irishness in my father's upbringing in the coal country of West Virginia, and there was definitely none in my childhood in the suburbs of the nation's capital. Indeed I don't recall ever once considering that my surname is Irish until after I became an adult.

Likewise there is no real history of music in my family. The only ancestor I know of on either side of the family who played an instrument was my great aunt Mary Hamilton – my grandmother's sister on my mother's side – who my mother recently told me would play by ear the same piano that sat unplayed in the front room of my grandmother's West Virginia farm house when we visited there in my childhood. The only singing would have been done in church. My mother was Protestant before she married my dad, otherwise there would have been no singing at all because Catholics don't sing much in church – and especially didn't when the Mass and all the music was in Latin. In seventh grade I had to take a music class and was faced with the choice of band or choir. I didn't want to sing, so I took band, started playing the clarinet, and found I had some aptitude for it. Playing in school bands through high school and college brought me to a love of classical music, and listening to a classical music radio station after I returned to the DC area to start work I heard a folk music program that featured a fair number of Irish songs. Something in those songs got to me, and it was through trying to sing them myself while playing a guitar that I found first the dancing, and then the tunes, where I remain immersed today. It was through the music that I found my Irishness.

I have two old black sticks that represent my Irishness and my place in the world of Irish traditional music. The first is a blackthorn walking stick, not elaborate at all, definitely not one of the fancy carved ones that get sold to tourists today. It belonged to my Grandfather Kerr's older sister Elizabeth, who entered the convent as Sister John Vincent a few years before my father was christened with the name John Vincent that he later passed on to me. Sister John Vincent was a young child when the Kerr family emigrated to America in 1895. I don't know if the stick came with them then, or if it was acquired later on. But it is definitely Irish, and it is old and has been well used over the years for the purpose it was cut.

The other old black stick is the Rudall and Rose flute that I play. Its serial number 4009 dates it to around 1840, and it was made in London to be played in an orchestra. The flute came to me through my friend, the flutemaker Patrick Olwell, who restored it. I have no idea if the flute has ever been to Ireland, or if anyone before Patrick ever played Irish tunes on it, but hundreds of simple system flutes of similar vintage are the reason Irish music is played on flute the way it is today. I have other flutes that are great for Irish music, most of them made by Patrick Olwell, but it's when I play the Rudall that the music feels most right.

One of my two old black sticks hangs as a decoration on my living room wall, as I have no need to use it for the reason it was cut. The other one sits in its case, until it comes out to play almost every day of my life. I think of something my father – not an appreciator of music at all, but someone who never complained when he had to endure my band concerts when I was a kid – once asked me after he and my mother came to the pub to watch a session I was playing in. *How do you know when to stop playing?* My answer was *We just know.* I likewise know that some day one of my two old black sticks will probably have to come off the wall to be used for its intended purpose, while the other one will have to sit in its case unplayed. But I hope that day is far away and that those two old black sticks stay in their current places for a good long time.

## THANKS

*Perhaps foolishly, I told no one I was writing this book and got no help with it from anyone along the way. So it might seem that I have no one to thank, but that couldn't be further from the truth. Without Brendan Mulvihill and Billy McComiskey, there would have been no Irish music scene in the Washington-Baltimore area for me to become part of. Without Celtic Thunder, and in particular Jesse and Terry Winch, there would have been no ceilis for me to step into. Without Michael Denney there would have been no Irish Festival to define the scene for fifteen years, and without Mick Moloney there would have been no Augusta Irish Week to provide my earliest foothold into the tradition. Without Patrick Olwell I would not have had flutes to play, and without Brian Gaffney there might not have been a session where I could play them. But beyond that, without the hundreds of other people who have become my friends while dancing to, playing or just simply enjoying Irish music, there would have been no point to any of it. Their names are sprinkled throughout this text, although I am sure I've neglected to mention some and for that I apologize. If there's ever a sequel, they will be in it. But since this one took over two years to write, no need to clear bookshelf space for that any time soon.*

Made in the USA
Lexington, KY
09 October 2013